WHAT READERS ARE SAYING ABOUT
THE MORNINGSIDE WORLD OF STUART MCLEAN

"Stuart McLean is CBC radio's Monday morning delight and mine. Now, in print, we all learn that he writes as enchantingly as he talks."

Peter Gzowski

"From The Miracle of Stanley Tavern to The Shocking Truth About Household Dust, every one of these luminous pieces is a joy to recall and a joy to read. For those of us who are Morningside addicts, Stuart McLean is a primal fix – Mondays are just not Mondays without him. My only fear, when I heard this book was in the works, was – yes, but can print deliver McLean's unique voice – the joyous rapport with Gzowski – the manic laughter – the breathtaking shocks of recognition? The answer, thank God, to all these questions, is yes. But a word of caution: these gems are like priceless souvenirs: don't leave them lying around or someone will try to steal them!"

Timothy Findley

"God bless Stuart McLean for his compassionate and witty glimpses of *good* people, in a world generally portrayed as going to the dogs."

Farley Mowat

WHAT THE REVIEWERS ARE SAYING:

"If our own daily lives are all too often grey because we've abandoned the child in us, McLean's world shines brightly: he sees and records the numinous in the prosaic."

The Edmonton Journal

". . . a good mixture of fun and sadness."

Gleaner (Fredericton)

"It's funny, it's invigorating and contains enough short vignettes of the Canadian way of life to keep you spellbound for many nights."

The Guardian (Brampton)

". . . reading *The Morningside World of Stuart McLean* is guaranteed to leave you better off, happier and more relaxed."

Star Phoenix (Saskatoon)

"McLean's style and subjects . . . soothe, comfort, draw one in . . ."

Preview (Montreal)

"Stuart McLean's quirky curiosity and keen sense of what makes a good story forces you to read on."

The Whig-Standard (Kingston)

"McLean's deceptively easy conversational style is that of a really first-class cracker-barrel raconteur."

Quill & Quire

PENGUIN BOOKS

The Morningside World of Stuart McLean

Stuart McLean was born and raised in Montreal. A long-time veteran of the Canadian Broadcasting Corporation, McLean worked on "Sunday Morning", CBC's national current affairs programme, and now appears Monday mornings with Peter Gzowski on "Morningside". Director of Broadcast Journalism at Ryerson Polytechnical Institute in Toronto, he was awarded an ACTRA Award for best radio documentarist and a B'nai Brith Award for Human Rights in Broadcast Journalism. He lives in Toronto with his wife and family.

THE MORNINGSIDE
WORLD OF

STUART McLEAN

Stuart McLean

Penguin Books

PENGUIN BOOKS

Published by the Penguin Group
Penguin Books Canada Ltd, 2801 John Street, Markham, Ontario,
Canada L3R 1B4
Penguin Books Ltd, 27 Wrights Lane, London W8 5TZ, England
Penguin Books USA Inc., 375 Hudson Street, New York, New York
10014, USA
Penguin Books Australia Ltd, Ringwood, Victoria, Australia
Penguin Books (NZ) Ltd, 182-190 Wairau Road, Auckland 10,
New Zealand

Penguin Books Ltd, Registered Offices: Harmondsworth,
Middlesex, England

First published in Viking by Penguin Books Canada Limited, 1989

Published in Penguin Books, 1990

1 3 5 7 9 10 8 6 4 2

Copyright © Stuart McLean, 1989

The following is used by permission:

From *Alligator Pie* by Dennis Lee. Used by permission of the
Canadian Publishers, McClelland and Stewart, Toronto.

Interior illustrations by Rosalind Goss.

YO-YO is a registered trademark of Canada Games Company
Limited.

Queries regarding radio broadcasting, motion picture, video
cassette, television and translation rights should be directed to the
Author's representative: Peter Livingston Associates, Inc., 1020
Bland Street, Halifax, Nova Scotia, Canada B3H 2S8.

Manufactured in Canada

Canadian Cataloguing in Publication Data

McLean, Stuart 1948-
The Morningside world of Stuart McLean

Essays from the CBC radio program Morningside.
ISBN 0-14-012608-2

I. Title. II. Title: Morningside (Radio program)
PS8575.L43M6 1990   C814'.54   C90-094838-8
PR9199.3.M33M6 1990

To my mother and father,
Pat and Andy McLean,
Montreal, Quebec

————————————

CONTENTS

THE MORNINGSIDE WORLD
OF STUART McLEAN

INTRODUCTION

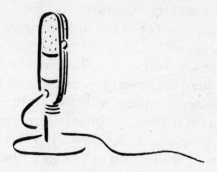

Almost every Monday morning for the past five years, I have risen early, dressed quietly and quickly in the darkness while my family slept, and driven sleepily along Bloor Street to the ramshackle rabbit warren, a stone's throw from Maple Leaf Gardens, that CBC Radio calls home. The Radio Building has seen better days. Once it was home to a toney private girls' school. But for all its present shabbiness it is, even before dawn, a friendly place to go. Made all the more friendly, perhaps, because it is home to Peter Gzowski and a wonderfully comfortable radio program called "Morningside". For five years I have been a regular on "Morningside". Every Monday morning I show up at the show's opening for a visit with Peter.

I am supposed to be a journalist.

In another part of my life I am actually paid as a professor of journalism. But I wouldn't want to claim that what Peter and I do together on Monday mornings is journalism. If I had to say anything, all I could say with certainty is that every Monday morning I appear with four pages of typed script hoping to tell a halfway interesting story.

This book contains some of my favourite stories.

A lot of people who hear me regularly say they are surprised to learn that I actually write my pieces down before I go on the radio. Well, I do. Our conversations, Peter's and mine, follow a script. Sort of.

Nearly all of what follows was written on Sunday evenings in the front room of our white stucco home in downtown Toronto. I like it in the front room. My new computer has a permanent place of its own built into the bookcase, complete with a neat little sliding shelf for the keyboard. I have my tape recorder on a table to my left, lots of space to spread out my notes, the telephone balanced on the arm of a chair within easy reach if I need distraction, and a big front window so I can keep watch on my neighbours as they trek down the street to buy milk from John at the corner store.

I write on Sunday nights because I am expected to appear early on Monday morning with my story in hand. There is nothing like a deadline to focus the mind. Every now and then the stories write themselves, and I spend the evening bouncing back and forth to my wife with smug progress reports. Other times I stumble up to bed as late as two or three in the morning, knowing that I have to get going in four hours.

Ever since the morning I slept in and my producer Nancy had to phone and wake me up, and I made it from bed to broadcast in twelve-and-a-half minutes, I carefully and obsessively set and check three separate alarm clocks before I go to sleep. I keep two beside me by the bed. The third is an oversized wind-up model that I borrowed from my neighbours Pete and Maggie a year or so ago. I keep it out of reach on the bureau and set it a half hour later than my other two alarms. It's my fail-safe clock. I imagine it to have an unpleasant and insistent buzzer, and the theory is, if I sleep in, this is the clock that will blast me to consciousness. Ever since I got it I have had no trouble waking up and always manage to turn it off before it rings.

I have written well over one hundred pieces for "Morningside". Over the years these stories have received a warm reception from a large part of the "Morningside" audience, though I am not really sure why they should. They are certainly not about important matters, at least, not in the way a newspaper editor might measure importance. Nor are they about prominent people or significant social trends. Often when people meet me they want to know where I get my ideas. Sometimes I wish I could offer some sort of logical explanation, but I am afraid I can't. The best I can do is say that there is something about these people and places that interested me. When I saw them or read about them, or when somebody wrote and told me about them, something inside me said, "that's a story." There is something about a restaurant that is serving alligator stew, or the event that we came to call the miracle of the Stanley Tavern, that I can't resist.

On the radio, each of these moments unfolded as a conversation between Peter Gzowski and me. And, yes, as he has said before, we enjoy these moments as much as it sounds. We both, you see, love a good story. And we both love radio.

As a boy I was brushed by the sunset days of radio's first golden era. Sadly, I missed "I Was a Communist for the FBI". But I do remember Red Ryder. Mostly I remember what radio meant to me as a teenager – alone in my bedroom with my radio and the top ten countdown. Afraid to come downstairs when I was called for supper in case I missed number one. After dark, when the sky filled up with radio, I would fiddle with the dial and try to pull in American stations. The goal in Montreal was to get a station from Buffalo with the lyrical call letters, WKBW. Each night DJ Joey Reynolds offered to initiate us into the Royal Order of the Night People, a ceremony that involved turning the lights off and melting a purple candle over the radio dial so when the wax hardened, not even our parents could switch stations.

I used to listen to an open line show hosted by the late and lamented Joe Pyne. Never one to let good manners get in the way of good radio, the nefarious Mr. Pyne would upbraid his listeners with his tart opinions and, if they should ever displease him, snap them brusquely off the air. I had never heard anything like it before, or since. Sometimes my pal Ross McGregor and I would set up our radios by our respective phones, call each other, and listen together. Joe Pyne was, for two thirteen-year-old boys from polite families, quite beyond belief.

At the other end of the spectrum there was, on Sunday night, a show called "Ask the Pastor". Pastor Johnson was, I think, a sort of penance, offered up by the station to atone for all the bile that Joe Pyne had inflicted on our city during the week.

The times and the programs may have changed, but my pleasure in radio hasn't. As an adult I discovered CBC. Working at CBC radio is like living in a small town. It is unpretentious, mildly eccentric, not particularly polished, and peopled by a cast of characters who don't spend a great deal of time with blow dryers. It is a quiet corner of the world and is the best of radio, for radio at its best is intimate. It is a companion. Someone you know, something to listen to.

Maybe I like radio because it is essentially democratic – a populist medium – and as such gives people a sense that they are heard.

Have you noticed that there is not a lot of violence on the radio? There are no rapes. No shootings. No sexual assaults. No Thundercats. No Captain Power. The South

African government has never accused anyone of staging a riot for radio.

There is also the question of pictures. Unlike television, radio is a visual medium and requires you to use your imagination. On the radio I can take you anywhere in time or space if you want to come with me. It all happens out in the ether.

That is the magic of radio – those fragile moments that are here for a moment and then shoot out into the ether and are . . . gone.

Well, here are some of them back again. Closer perhaps to the way they came out of my typewriter on Sunday night than the way they came out of your radio. Touched up here and there because now they are meant to be read, while before they were meant to be read aloud.

I have resisted the urge to update anything. Things change too fast these days and, quite frankly, if the Coldwater Municipal Phone Company has gone and sold out to Bell Canada, I for one, don't want to know about it. I want to believe that during alligator season I could still drop in at The Other Cafe and order a plate of Alligator Stew. I know that Ernie is still selling hot dogs every day at Ryerson. I'm going to assume that Clark the waiter is still slinging draft at the Stanley Tavern. That's the way I found him, and that's the way he's going to stay.

August, 1989
Lac Marois, Quebec

THE MIRACLE OF THE STANLEY TAVERN

As citizens of the twentieth century, we share a lot of things modern that them what went before us done without. We have, to name just a few modern wonders, the Veg-o-matic, Naugahyde, Styrofoam and saccharin (or don't they allow that anymore?). It's hard to keep up. And, of course, there are those little scratch-and-sniff strips that come in the fancy fashion magazines. These technological advances, wondrous as they are, have not, sadly, come without cost. Something won, something lost.

One thing we have given up on is the miracle. Ever since the Industrial Revolution and the emergence of scientific reasoning, there just have not been a lot of miracles. Yes, *Newsweek* did carry the story when Christ's face appeared on the Texan tortilla, but they didn't treat it seriously. If they had *really* believed it, they would have put it on the cover, not in the little box at the back of the magazine. I have always thought it is a shame that we have given up this sense of wonder from our lives. Which is why I was so excited when my friend John Weldon called to tell me about the Miracle of the Stanley Tavern.

The Stanley Tavern is, not surprisingly, on Stanley Street. Like most good Montreal taverns, the "Stan" is small. It is more like a wide corridor than a bar. It is brightly lit and has serious wooden chairs. It is an elbows-on-the-table sort of place where you can order Pig Knuckle Ragout. And, of course, beer. The beer comes from a serving island near the back of the tavern. In case you haven't figured it out already, the Stan is the kind of place that has regular customers – lots of them.

Kevin McCracken and Chris Hinton are two regulars at the Stanley. It is their custom to stop in for a few drafts every Thursday night after their regular squash game. On the Thursday night in question (Thursday, February 27, 1986), Kevin and Chris settled down at their regular table around nine o'clock. Thursday night is not normally a busy night at the Stan and, as usual, Clark was the only waiter on the floor.

If you have ever been a regular customer at a Montreal tavern, you know the peculiar ritual that surrounds the act of ordering beer. Waiters do not, as a habit, come to the tables to take orders. They cast their eyes, rather than their bodies, around the room. When a waiter and a customer make eye contact, the customer raises his hand in the air displaying one, two or perhaps four fingers. The number of fingers held aloft is taken as a request for the equivalent number of draft beers.

When Kevin made eye contact with Clark on the Thursday night in question, Kevin was, as usual, waving four fingers.

Now, Clark is a good waiter. Which is to say he has both good eyesight and fast feet. So when nearly five minutes had passed and the four beers hadn't arrived, both Kevin and Chris were puzzled enough to wonder what was going on. When Kevin turned to look at the back of the bar, this is what he saw:

"Well, we saw Clark just pounding on the tap. There was somebody else standing beside him, and they were both standing there, sort of quizzically staring at the tap, and Clark is making these great body gestures, shrugging his shoulders and waving his hands, and this was unusual because Clark doesn't usually have too much to say. You can usually read what's going on with him quite easily. But there he was just hammering on that tap, and every now and then the lights in the bar were flickering on and off. You know, the back lights would go out, the front lights would go out, and Clark was really quite upset."

Clark had cause to be upset. He was standing in front of the lever he had used to pull Kevin and Chris's four drafts. The four honey-coloured glasses of beer were on the counter beside him. The lever was back in the off position. But foaming golden beer was still pouring out of the spigot and, as Clark remembers it, no matter what he did, it wouldn't stop.

"There was a flood of beer. Beer was flowing into the sink and onto the floor. There was a flood around my feet. There was just beer coming out both taps like a flood. It was like water all over me. All over the place. There's nothing that could receive that amount of beer, so it just overflowed all over the place. At first I was filling glasses, but before I knew it I had no more glasses left."

Having filled all the glasses at hand, and still confronted by the cascade of beer sloshing onto the floor of the Stanley Tavern, Clark the waiter looked wildly around and dashed into the tavern kitchen, reappearing moments later swinging two huge soup cauldrons. He shoved one of them under the gushing spigot and madly mopped the floor in the ensuing lull. The cauldron, however, filled up alarmingly quickly, and in moments Clark had to hump it from under the tap and shove the empty one in its place.

Now it is important to remember that Clark was the only waiter on duty this particular Thursday night, so at this point none of the thirty or forty customers on hand had been served for close to ten minutes. Everyone in the tavern therefore watched in horror as Clark struggled across the floor with the cauldron full of draft beer and . . . tipped-it-down-the-sink. Kevin was almost paralysed.

"I mean, it's one of those things you never want to see again. We watched him struggle with that big heavy cauldron that's so full of beer that it's hard to carry, and then saw him totter over to the sink and dump it out. Just to see that amount of nice, rich, white suds going down was . . . it was awful. Just the tip and the slushing of the suds down the drain was a really sickening sight. And he did this probably three times. Before long he had other people – customers – bringing the buckets to him as they filled, but they still couldn't keep up with it."

The tavern had begun to resemble the climactic scene from Walt Disney's *Sorcerer's Apprentice*. The room was awash with beer buckets and mops when Clark (who is playing the role of Mickey Mouse here) yelled that he was going to the basement where there was, he said, a "master switch". Clark disappeared through the kitchen, and the customers who had been helping him continued to monitor the spill. In what seemed like the blink of an eye,

Clark burst back into the room. His face dropped when he looked at the spigot and saw that the beer was still flowing. He had failed. Chris remembers this as the moment when Clark began to panic.

"I guess he's fearing for his job at this point because Clark seemed just consumed with trying to find some way of shutting the thing off. He was walking around with a pair of pliers, just hitting every switch he could find. The tap was on one side of the floor, and the switch – the electrical panel – was directly behind him. He thwacked the pump as hard as he could, and it wouldn't shut off, so he turned around and raced down all the switches and tried everything once or twice, or a dozen times. But nothing seemed to have any effect on the tap whatsoever."

At this juncture in our story it is perhaps worthwhile to pause and enumerate exactly what Clark has done so far to stop the flow of beer. He has
- put the lever of the spigot in the off position;
- hit the spigot with his hand, much the way you'd hit a vending machine that has misbehaved;
- hit the spigot with his pliers;
- used his key that is supposed to trigger the safety switch;
- killed all the power in the bar, plunging it into darkness in an attempt to kill the electric pump;
- and, while others manned the soup cauldrons upstairs, gone to the basement and wildly pulled at the hoses that run between the kegs of beer, hoping, in vain, to cut the flow.

None of these things worked. And while all this went on, the clients, including Chris and Kevin, sat sort of slack-jawed, sort of stunned, as they watched gallons of beer being poured down the drain.

That was when Clark the waiter, who couldn't figure out what to do next, announced that anyone who wanted could start drinking the beer for free. He made his announcement and then disappeared once again into the basement, with his pliers, leaving everyone alone upstairs. Chris says he'll never forget that moment.

"Well, people were sitting there with a look of disbelief on their faces wondering if it could be really true, or was it just a mirage. We really wouldn't have been surprised, I don't think, if the Candid Camera crew had stepped out from behind the walls at that point. But they didn't. It wasn't a practical joke. It was a moment of divine intervention. I'm sure of it. Because there was nothing they could do – turning the power off, turning the taps off. If they'd blown the building up I think the tap would have continued to flow. There was nothing that could be done. It had to be divine intervention. I mean, this is the province of miracles of this nature. I think everybody was hoping for such a miracle when it first started, but to see it continue and go on and on . . . people's expressions lit up. It was very joyful in there."

Beer flowed unabated from the draft tap at the Stanley Tavern for over thirty-five minutes that night. But not a drop hit the floor after Clark handed the spigot over to his customers. By the time the fountain finally dried up, there was a cauldron on every table and people were dipping glasses into their tubs of draft as if that was the way you drank beer in Montreal. No one had to buy a beer between 9:17 and closing.

When closing time eventually arrived, there was much embracing and shaking of hands between tables. Hard times bring people together. There was general agreement in the tavern that everyone there had witnessed a miracle. But those who stayed until the bitter end wanted a better explanation. Why had such a thing happened? And why on that night, in that place?

Just before closing time, Kevin sensed an explanation surfacing.

"At this point we figured, there's got to be something more to this whole miracle thing than is meeting the eye. Well, I should point out that on the TV that night there were clips of old hockey games from the sixties. Clips that were highlighting Jacques Plante, who had sadly died earlier that day. And it just sort of all clicked in at once that there's Jacques Plante, probably one of the most eccentric characters who has ever played for the Montreal Canadiens. The tap was running freely; we were watching some of the greatest hockey ever played in the history of the game. And we came to figure out why this was happening at the *Stanley* Tavern, too, being the Stanley Cup, of course, and everything seemed to fit – Jacques Plante, the beer taps open. Everything fell into place. The puzzle was solved. It was quite clear then and it's quite clear now. It *was* a miracle. A moment of passing. A moment to remember."

Well. Yes. Indeed. Who is going to argue or say it ain't so? It happened exactly the way I've told it, and why not? I submit that tavern miracles are the perfect miracle for our age – small, secular and above all scientifically verifiable. There are probably still a lot of tavern miracles not used up yet. It is largely an unexplored area. I am sure that more will come to light, but this is the only one I know about to date.

MYSTERIES OF THE WOODEN PENCIL

There are many reasons to cherish the wooden pencil. Let me begin by proposing that pencils foster good fellowship. As a rule, people do not feel possessive about pencils. Them that's got . . . give. Pencils wander mysteriously in and out of our lives. Chances are if you have a pencil in your pocket right now, you would be hard pressed to say where it came from. Pencils are both loyal and dependable. If, in the autumn, you were to forget one at the back of a dresser drawer at the cottage, you can count on it being there in the spring. And you can depend on it to work, first try.

Pencils do not have big egos. They do not mind being erased, and who among us can say that? Pencils are cheap, they have no moving parts, you can still buy them unwrapped, and they will not leak in your pocket. They are perhaps the last tool you have in your house that you can service yourself. You do not have to send your pencils out to be sharpened. In both form and function I submit that the wooden pencil has achieved perfection.

And, I am happy to report, there is a lot more to pencils

than meets the eye. This I discovered from the man who makes more wooden pencils than anyone else in Canada. As far as Canada is concerned, he is Mr Pencil. His name, pleasingly, is Vic Steele. His business card says President of Faber-Castell Canada Inc. It was from Vic that I learned what I have fondly come to think of as the mysteries of the wooden pencil.

The mysteries begin with just that, the wood. I sat in Vic's office and listened, somewhat miffed, as he explained to me that every pencil he makes – in fact every pencil that is manufactured in Canada – is made with American wood. Vic says he and his competitors import all the wood that goes into Canadian pencils.

"We manufacture pencils from a tree called the California incense cedar. It is grown in the northern parts of California, and it's essentially a bad tree. It's rotten in the middle and it's filled with knots and crevices. Until twenty or twenty-five years ago, it had no commercial value. It wasn't even harvested in the forest. Trees just fell over when they got rotten, and that was the end of them. But pencil manufacturers discovered if they cut those logs up enough times, they would find some beautiful pieces of cedar with straight grain. Remember, the pencil industry is one of the few users of wood who don't require their lumber to be six and eight feet long. We only need seven and one quarter inches, and it's obvious that if you cut this tree up enough, you will find some beautiful pieces of seven inch cedar. That's why we buy California incense cedar. The cedar and the pine in Canada are just too good. They have too many other commercial uses. It would be too expensive to use Canadian cedar to make a pencil."

Now, I don't feel that way. As far as I am concerned, no

wood is too good for a pencil.

But I suspected that Vic held the solution to a more intriguing mystery. A question I had puzzled over from time to time. Wherever he got the wood from, how, I wondered, did Vic get the lead into the middle of the pencil? Some years ago I had decided that they drilled a hole down the middle and dropped the lead into place. I was wrong.

Imagine a block of wood the size of a pound of butter. Now take a knife and scalp the pound of butter. Cut a slice off the top of the block of wood about one-quarter inch thick. What you should have is a piece of California incense cedar that, from the top, looks like a pound of butter, but is only one-quarter inch thick. Pretend that you are a farmer and that you want to plant nine rows of corn in that block of wood. What you will need is a router, so get it out and drill nine furrows down the length of the block. Next take nine pieces of pencil lead and lay one down in each of the furrows. Now get another piece of California incense cedar, the same size, place it on top of the one where you have laid the lead and glue it in place, so you have a kind of lead sandwich. If you take that lead sandwich and cut between the pieces of lead, you will end up with nine pencils. Every pencil, it turns out, is actually two pieces of wood glued together. If you look down near the point of a freshly sharpened pencil, you can often see the line where the two pieces of wood meet.

In Canada, once they have shaped the pencils round, for comfort, they paint them yellow. And that is the next mystery. Because no one, not even Vic Steele, knows why. All anyone knows is that Canadians want their pencils yellow. Once, Vic thought it would be a clever marketing ploy to distinguish Faber-Castell pencils by painting them different colours. But as Vic explained, things didn't exactly pan out when he started to mess with tradition. What happened?

"Well, in a word, people rejected them. Canadians expect their pencils to be yellow. They don't want them coloured differently. Pencils have been yellow since we were children, and everyone expects them to stay that way. People made it clear that they don't want us to tamper with their expectations and, being marketers, we don't. If they want to buy yellow pencils, that's what we give them. You know, well over 90 percent of our black-lead pencils are painted yellow. We have a few that we colour. We use hot colours, and so on, because we think that younger children will be attracted to them. But the North American market has largely rejected colours on black-lead pencils. Now, that's not the case in the rest of the world. In Asia and most of Europe, pencils are striped, spotted and decorated in a variety of colours. There are almost no yellow pencils in Europe and the Orient. Yellow is a North American phenomenon."

It is a phenomenon that is taken seriously. Every pencil in Vic Steele's plant gets at least ten coats of paint before it goes out the door. The pencils clatter along a conveyor belt and are shot under pressure through buckets of yellow paint. After they have received their requisite coats of yellow, they get a couple of coats of lacquer to boot. The lacquer is what makes pencils shiny. Vic told me that even with all this care, the Japanese and Europeans turn their noses up at North American pencils. Our pencils, he says, are not lustrous enough for their taste.

The eraser is another peculiarity to the North American pencil. In Europe and Japan, people do not want erasers. In fact, you can't give pencils away if they have erasers on them. Nor can you sell those little arrow-shaped erasers that are meant to be slipped onto the end of a pencil. It seems that in Europe and Japan a pencil is a pencil and an eraser is an eraser. In North America we are a lot more casual about wiping things out.

Europeans and North Americans do share one thing when it comes to pencils – the code letters "H" and "B" to catalogue the relative blackness of the lead.

"Those letters H and B come from one of the founders of our company. Back in the nineteenth century he invented lead degrees, which is the process of putting more or less graphite into a pencil so that it will be more or less black. He then decided to grade pencils by degrees of hardness and softness. He called the hard degrees "hart" (German for hard), and they became the "H" grades. He called the soft grades "blei" (German for lead), and they became the "B" grades. The one we use most often, HB, is the one in the middle. It's neither hard nor soft, so it's hart-blei."

Somehow it reassures me to think that the pencil hasn't fundamentally changed from the days of my youth. The pencil my son uses at school is the same as the one both my dad and I used. There are not many products you can say that about. Like many of us, today's pencil is a little thinner than its forefathers. But that is all. When I was a boy they would cut eight pencils from each block of California incense cedar. Today they cut nine. Over the past twenty years all the pencil research and development has thankfully been focused on the manufacturing process. No one, thank God, has busied themselves trying to redesign the pencil. They have just been trying to make them more efficiently. Which is why you can still buy pencils cheap. For some reason the cheapest place to buy pencils in Canada today is in Alberta, where in certain drugstores you can get one for a nickel.

Sadly, there may be change on the horizon. Vic Steele

told me that Faber-Castell has begun to spend R and D dollars on the pencil itself. They have been looking at the eraser.

"There's a family of erasers that have come out of the plastic industry in the last twenty or twenty-five years, which are vinyl. They're plastic but they are very good. They are less abrasive and do a better job generally than a comparable rubber eraser. But they are expensive. Our idea is to try and find a way to put a vinyl eraser into a pencil. The problem is that vinyl in that size tends to break. It doesn't hold up. So we've got a problem with breakage. We think it will be to the customer's advantage if we had a good vinyl eraser in the tip of the pencil."

It may be to the customer's advantage, but I don't see it. For one thing, they would be the wrong colour – white – to maintain, as Vic puts it, "product differentiation." And I just don't think white goes with yellow. Not as well as pink, anyway.

Vic is worried that this might be a moot point. He is concerned that the new inexpensive mechanical pencils are going to eat into the market that, until now, the wooden pencil has had all to itself. But the mechanical pencil has a long way to go. In Canada every man, woman and child uses about seven pencils a year. And we sharpen them 2.8 times each before moving to the next. That's a lot of pencils. The mystery is who buys them all. Certainly not me. They just seem to arrive when I need them, and depart just as mysteriously.

ROLLER RINK REUNION

When you came in from the parking lot, you stepped into a small foyer and there were two escalators. Nothing else. One was marked CURLING and the other ROLLER SKATING. Without hesitating, I stepped onto the escalator marked ROLLER SKATING.

This was my first visit to our local roller-skating palace. Known now as the Terrace, it was once the largest hockey rink in the Dominion. In those days it was called the Mutual Street Arena, and ten thousand fans used to cram in to watch teams like the Montreal Maroons play the hometown Toronto Arenas. It was from Mutual Street that Foster Hewitt chanted his first live play-by-play. And in the summer, when the ice was gone, hockey would be replaced by the gruelling six-day bicycle races that were popular at the time.

Still standing, the arena is now tucked into the shadow of a Sears warehouse, a stone's throw from Maple Leaf Gardens. When they renovated twenty-five years ago, they gutted the whole building, so now, if you drive there, you actually park your car where the ice used to be. In fact, if you cared about these things (which, incidentally, I do) and took the time to figure it out (which I didn't), you could probably park smack on the spot that used to be centre ice.

They built two new floors above the old ice level when they renovated. On the second floor they built curling rinks, which is, I guess, the way you upgrade ice. And up where the cheap seats used to be, up in the rafters where the smoke used to dance in the lights, they built roller skating. They also built the foyer with the two escalators – the one marked CURLING, and the one marked ROLLER SKATING that was tugging me towards an evening I'll never forget.

Something must have happened on the way up because at the top, when I stepped off the escalator, it was suddenly 1956. The lights were dim and there was a soft waltz playing and everyone was paired up and waltzing on roller skates. Touch dancing. Standing in the twinkling light, I understood immediately why you would want to call a room like this a palace and not a rink. I was so bewitched that I didn't see the man standing beside me wearing skates. He was about seventy years old. When I did notice him, we nodded politely at each other the way you nod at someone you don't know. Then we both smiled and started talking. He told me it was a special night – a reunion for people who had skated regularly at the Terrace over the past fifty years. As he talked I was thinking how beautiful the room was – which was really what he was trying to tell me, as he nodded at the skaters.

"That's one thing I never learnt to do was waltz. When I was a kid, all I wanted to do was go like hell. There was a rink in Cincinnati I was in one night, and there was a thousand couples waltzing. It was a great big huge rink. And the ceiling was stars twinkling.

And at the far end of the rink there was a big face of a moon. And the moon would blink its eye every so often, and they had music that was suspended from the ceiling in this glass bubble. There was a band up there, and they would climb down a ladder during intermission; they had trombone traps and trumpets. Believe me, the beat that that there music put out – if you never roller skated a day in your life, you had to keep in time to that music."

"It sounds like it was a night to fall in love," I said.

"That's where I met my wife, in a roller rink. And we've been happily married for about forty-four years. So there's nothing wrong with that."

The dance ended, and my companion nodded and skated away. I watched him coast around the room and suddenly found myself thinking about the formal dances at the Lac Marois Country Club. It was 1962. The Andy Snee Orchestra always played at the formal dances. They were four guys who sat behind blue-and-white wooden music stands that had "Andy Snee Orchestra" written in silver script across the front. I stood there in the roller rink remembering the Paul Jones dance where everyone changed partners and you didn't have to ask a girl to dance. Thinking about that made me think about the night Donald Moore and I went down to the boys' change room to try to figure out what you were supposed to do when you were doing the Twist, after you had twisted back and forth for a while. It was dark down in the change room, which was kind of an outhouse-like structure built by the lake, and I remember telling Donald that I had the back and forth part down all right, but there had to be something more to it than that. What did he figure came next?

And then suddenly I felt from far away the anxiety that

used to sweep over me as the last dance loomed closer and closer. I remembered trying to find the courage to ask Georgie Murphy for the last dance. I would have these long conversations with myself. I would watch David Struthers behind the counter at the tuck shop and promise myself that the first time someone ordered a cream soda, the first time that David pulled a cream soda out of the cooler, I would go and ask Georgie Murphy if I could have the last dance. And then I would see David Struthers dip his arm up to the elbow into the cooler and pull out a wet cream soda, and I would dissolve. Black cherry, I'd say to myself. I'll ask her on the black cherry.

These were the things I was thinking about as I watched them waltz on their roller skates at the Terrace. And, as I watched, I found myself nodding again, this time to a woman beside me who, like my last companion, was easily over seventy. She, too, I learned, had met her husband at a roller rink – at the Terrace, in fact. And, like me, she was thinking about the old days.

"Tell me about the night you met your husband," I asked her. "Was it love at first sight?"

"It was on my part," she said, looking at the ceiling. "I don't know if it was on his part. But my girlfriend introduced us, and I took him away from another woman, which made it even nicer."

"Right there that night on the rink?"

"Right there. She had her claws into him and I said no way."

"How did you do that?" I asked.

"I used my charm," she said with a twinkle.

As the night wore on, it seemed as if every second person I talked to had met their wife or husband or their first boyfriend or girlfriend at the rink. And those who didn't

have love stories wanted to tell me about other con-
quests. My favourite, I think, was Len Harris. Thirty
years ago CHUM Radio, in Toronto, boosted its power
up to 5,000 watts. As a publicity stunt they invited To-
rontonians to drop by the station and try to open a safe
in which they had locked 5,000 one-dollar bills. Anyone
who showed up at the station got 60 seconds at the
lock.

You know who Len Harris is?

"I'm the guy who opened the safe back in 1958," he
said proudly.

"What was the combination?" I asked, smiling.
Len didn't miss a beat.

"92-47-61."

"What did it feel like when it opened?" I wondered.

"When it opened it felt like somebody had turned
around and, I don't know, I guess maybe poured a
can of gas on me and lit a match and said *burn*.
Because my whole body just lit up with energy or
fever or whatever you want to call it. I could feel the
blood surging inside me. It was one of the greatest
moments of my life. I went home, I paid my mom's
bills off, then went out and bought myself a brand-
new motorcycle and drove it all over hell's half acre
for a good year and a half before I turned around
and sold it and settled down."

One of the things about doing what I do for a living is that
I find myself talking to people I might not ordinarily talk
to. If I had wandered into the Terrace without my tape
recorder, I could have skated on the rink all night and
never known anything about the people around me. As a
journalist I am "allowed" to approach people and ask
them all sorts of questions. And, because I'm a

journalist, they mostly answer. I often find myself thinking, "My God, I could never make this up." And I think I
can safely say that if I had sat down to script the rest of
the night, I could never have come up with the next
chapter, which happened near the snack bar.

You can skate, you see, to the snack bar. You can also
skate to the seats that are beside the snack bar. That's
where I was sitting when a middle-aged woman came
rolling off the rink rather quickly and pirouetted right in
front of me – jumped up in the air, hung there suspended
for an instant, spun around so her modest blue skirt
flared out, and then landed without breaking stride in the
seat beside me.

"Quite a move," I said, smiling.

"I'm experienced at this," she replied, laughing,
"I've been coming here forty years."

"My goodness," I exclaimed. "How has it
changed?"

"How has it changed?" she said. "It hasn't
changed. I have."

"How have you changed?" I wondered.

"I used to be a man," she said nonchalantly.

I didn't know what to say, so I didn't say anything. I sat on
the bench smiling at her stupidly as my mind raced.
I was trying to think of an appropriate response. But I
wasn't thinking as a human being. I was thinking as a
performer. What do I say into my tape recorder, I wondered, so I can play this interview on the radio? What can I
say so that I sound clever? I am not particularly proud to
admit this, but that is what I was thinking. And because I
didn't like that so terribly much, I turned off my machine
and talked to Christine for a while just like I talked to
everyone else.

She told me that she had come to the Terrace for over

thirty years as a man and then one day started showing up as a woman. Now, I have to say that in many ways Christine still looks quite masculine, like a man dressed as a woman. For a while I watched her talking to other regulars – bus drivers, plumbers, an engineer and some others who had known her as John and now knew her as Christine. As I watched the easy bantering, which was all so normal, low-key and unaffected, I was struck by what a great capacity for tolerance and change and love we all have when we don't feel threatened. Then I met the skating instructor.

The skating instructor wasn't wearing skates. He was leaning against the boards watching everyone waltz with the same faraway look in his eye that I'd had at the beginning of the night. The lights were low and the music was soft and you could almost see the stars twinkling the way they had that night in Cincinnati.

"You taught some of these people to waltz," I said.

He nodded.

"Which pupil are you proudest of?"

He searched the floor and pointed to a couple waltzing elegantly at the far end of the rink.

"That guy," he said, pointing.

The man he was pointing at was balding, wearing a suit and had a neatly trimmed beard. Maybe he was a lawyer or a manager of a store.

"I'm really proud of John for the simple reason that when he came down here he was a bum. He was a wino, he really was. There he was, a drunk lacing up his skates, and we couldn't kick him out because he had paid his admission. He could barely stand up. Now look at him. In time to the music, oh, he's looking good. Like there are some kids here that have gone on to competitions – provincial champion-ships, you know? But I'm proudest of John. Here he comes round again, and he's doing great. Posture is good. He's got a very inexperienced partner. You can tell that by the way she is skating backwards. But he's doing good.

"And he used to be a wino, really?" I asked incredulously, looking at the elegant man on the floor.

"Really. Literally. Because when he first came in we thought, oh, my God, look who's coming in, and we used to make fun of him wanting to learn how to skate. But because he paid his admission and he got a pair of skates on and he tried, hey, I'll help him. The other ones didn't want to touch him, because he wasn't the cleanest-looking person. But what the heck if he wants to learn how to skate I'll give him a shot. And, Jesus, he was great. Who would have believed it, hey? I wouldn't have believed it, I wouldn't have believed it. But he was determined to turn his life around, and he did."

We stood there quietly by the rink and watched John. After some time I noticed that the lights were gradually getting brighter, and the music was changing. A younger crowd was moving in. Street kids. The disco crowd. T-shirts and leather. I decided it was time for me to go. I didn't want this new crowd intruding on the world I had found. I went back to the snack shop to put my things together. I packed my recorder into its case and headed out. As I left I saw Christine. She waved and came over.

"So how do you think I am going to do?" she asked. "How do you think I'll do in my new life as a woman?"

I stopped and looked her in the eye.

"I think you'll do fine," I said.

Then I turned and went home. When I got there I crawled into bed with my wife. I first met her at one of those dances at the Lac Marois Country Club when I was thirteen.

A FEW KIND WORDS ABOUT BARBER SHOPS

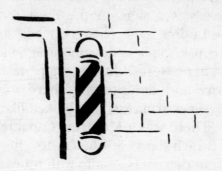

Like many men, I forsook the barber shop sometime during the 1970s. I am not proud of the fact today, but I began to frequent one of those so-called "stylists", where they clip your wallet as well as your head. I am not sure what finally turned me around. It might have been the music, or the fact that my stylist, who never looked old enough to be living away from home, seemed to be someone different every time I went. It also could have been the decor. From the outside it was difficult to tell the difference between the place where I was having my hair cut and the store where they sold the gourmet goat's milk cheese. You can say whatever you want about an old-fashioned barber shop, but you'll never mix one up with a cheese store. I think that's what did it.

When I was young, my mom and dad took my brother Al and me to the West End Barber Shop. The West End was renowned amongst my friends because Doug Harvey was said to go there to have his hair cut. In my younger life I only really wanted two things – white bucks like Pat Boone and a brushcut like Doug Harvey. My mother said my feet were too narrow for white bucks and my hair would never stand up like Doug Harvey's hair if they cut it that short. What can you say to that?

I don't know if the West End Barber Shop is still there. I do know that it is still etched in my mind. There was a plant in the window that was never watered, yet never died. There was a sign on the door that said, simply, "Wildroot Lotion". There were magazines that taught you how to make a plane in your garage that you could fly to work. There were ashtrays on pedestals that defied both gravity and description. There were red leather chairs with silver arm rests that looked like they had come off a ship. There was a Montreal Canadiens calendar on the wall (which lent substance to the Doug Harvey rumour), and there was a radio with tubes on the counter. In the back there was a room where all the hair went, in the front mysterious drawers where the barbers kept mysterious things. They didn't have layered haircuts or feathered haircuts. They had short and medium.

These days I go to Byron, who has the chair beside Gus, in a storefront barber shop on Bloor Street, enigmatically named "Gus The Other Barber". I can walk to Gus's barber shop from my home. Gus has been cutting hair at the same chair since 1959.

"I've been twenty-five years in this place, and I still have customers that started with me twenty-five years ago. I have kids five, six, seven years old – kids who had their first haircut here. And today I can see these kids – they are men, they have families – and they bring their own kids. And this makes me feel good to see the same people after so many years, you know, the same customers. Of course I have new ones also. It makes me happy. They know me, and they know my family after so many years. They tell me their secrets, their problems, I tell them mine. Sometimes

I help them, too. A psychiatrist was here not long ago and he was listening – I was trying to talk to a customer about a problem he had – and after the customer left he says, 'You know, I'm a psychiatrist. It looks like you are doing the same job as me.' "

They have everything at Gus's barber shop – the leather strap, the lilac water, the lather machine, and lined up on the counter the tall thin bottles full of phosphorescent liquids. My favourite is what I call the Green Stuff. Byron rubs the Green Stuff into your hair at the end of your haircut. But before you get the Green Stuff, you follow a ritual that never changes. First you swing into your chair by stepping up onto the pedestal thing that looks like it has been pried off an old escalator. Then Byron covers you, sprays you down and gets to work with the scissors and comb. Next he uses the thinners, the clippers, the shaving cream, the straight razor and finally, just before the talcum powder, you get the Green Stuff.

At first nothing special happens when Byron massages the mysterious liquid into your hair, but about five minutes after you stand up, your head feels as if it is about to ignite. It feels as if a small thermonuclear device has gone off and blown the top of your scalp away. One day while Byron was brushing errant hairs off the back of my coat, I peeked at the label and read that the Green Stuff was really something called "Sage-On Head Rub". I liked it so much that I went to the Barber Supply Company and bought myself a bottle.

The only disadvantage to the Green Stuff is that your head smells like a bowl of peppermints for about two days after you use it. I think that's a small price to pay for pleasure. My wife disagrees, and I am not allowed to use the bottle I brought home. Anticipating Sage-On Head Rub makes my trips to see Byron all the more wonderful.

I like going to the barber on Saturday, which happens to be the busiest day of the week. Sometimes on Saturday you can see the man who comes and collects all the cut hair from the room in the back. Gus told me he takes it home and uses it in his garden as fertilizer. The TV is usually on and there is usually soccer on the TV. I don't mind if there is a line-up. In fact, that's just fine with me. If there is a line-up I go next door to the pool hall and get a coffee to go for me, and maybe for Gus or Byron or Leslie if any of them want one. I bring the coffee back and sit and talk with whoever is there. Not that I know anyone there. Most of Gus's customers are Greek, and we talk about things that I know very little about.

There are three big topics of conversations at Gus's.

Soccer.

What Gus should do if he wins the lottery.

And, lately, women.

Gus is thinking about adding one more chair to the store (there are three, would there be room for a fourth?) and hiring . . . a woman. Not that women never come in. You often see mothers standing anxiously over their little boys, and once or twice I have seen a woman having her hair cut. But it's not a regular sort of occurrence. A woman in one of Gus's chairs is something that you notice, the way you might notice a woman driving a steamroller on a construction site. You just don't see that every day.

Gus says that there is money in perms and tints, but he is nervous about changing the character of his store and has been asking everyone what they think of the idea.

"A lot of people, they don't mind, but quite a few don't really like the idea of women here. They feel comfortable the way it is. We talk about sports, politics, sometimes we scream a little bit. It's nice, but if we have ladies here it's not going to be so easy.

You can't express your feelings and your ideas when ladies are here. No matter where you go you are only going to find a few places like mine – just a barber shop, right? And people get used to it. But I don't know, people change with time. We'll have to see."

People may change, but change doesn't sit easy with those of us who love barbers. There are enduring rituals that happen to a man's head in a barber shop. The most important one is the moment they put the shaving cream on the back of your neck. It is a ceremony that signals the end of the haircut is near. The barber lathers up your neck and takes a straight razor and exquisitely sculpts the line where hair meets skin.

You don't get the shaving cream part when you are a kid. You have to be old enough. And the first time it happens is a mysterious and wonderful rite of passage. You are suddenly . . . a man. I know a boy who got the shaving cream part for the first time last month.

"I thought the haircut was over, and I was just waiting for him to take off the cape that keeps the hair from going all over your clothes. But my barber, Leslie, reached over to a 1950s-looking machine, pushed a lever and filled his hand with cream – shaving cream. And Gus came over and joked about giving me a Mohawk, and we all laughed. But I still didn't know what was going to happen. Then Leslie got a sort of razorish comb-looking device and scraped across my skull. I didn't feel anything; it didn't hurt or anything. It didn't look any different, but it made me feel different. I guess I felt . . . older."

It costs nine dollars, plus tip, to have your hair cut at Gus's. And for nine dollars not only do you get your hair cut, but Gus or Leslie or Byron will whisk you through time and plop you back wherever you want to go. They take me to Sherbrooke Street in 1956. To the West End Barber Shop. It's a great way to spend a Saturday morning.

You know when you are walking down the street and you see those barbers sitting alone in their shops, waiting in their chairs, waiting in their empty stores. You have probably asked yourself what they are doing there.

They are waiting for you.

Go back to your barber.

WELCOME TO ZANZIBAR GARDENS

I stood at the top of the stairs and listened to the chatter spilling through the open apartment door at the end of the dim corridor. I decided no one would hear me knocking anyway, so I shrugged and walked towards the conversation.

There were maybe twenty people standing in the dining-room, holding drinks and eating hot dogs and then, as they noticed me, falling quiet.

I realized I was staring, but I couldn't help it. I couldn't believe what I was looking at.

A man in his early thirties, wearing a dark sweater and dark pants, pushed forward.

"You're Stuart McLean," he half asked and half announced.

"Yes," I said, holding out my hand.

"I'm Michael Birthelmer," he said smiling. "Welcome to Zanzibar Gardens."

Walking into Michael J. Birthelmer's life is like walking through the Looking-Glass into a truly Canadian alternate reality based on, what else, hockey. Zanzibar Gardens is such an astonishing concept that when I first heard about it I assumed it only existed in Michael Birthelmer's imagination. What makes it most remarkable is that it has crawled out of his mind. And I was staring at it.

The Gardens itself is a huge replica of a professional hockey arena. The ice surface is a four-by-eight piece of plywood which has been painted white and urethaned and Varathaned so that it looks just like the ice surface in Maple Leaf Gardens. The plywood ice is surrounded on all sides by a four-foot-high Styrofoam arena filled with twelve thousand tiny little cardboard people. Each one of them has been cut by hand from a magazine and glued carefully into a Styrofoam seat. Ronald Reagan is in the crowd. So are Chuck and Di, a lot of tiny women in lingerie and, up in the end Greens, the Beatles. They all sit there patiently and watch what happens on the plywood rink. What they see is almost beyond description.

On the ice, Michael Birthelmer gets down on his hands and knees and, using Shirriff hockey coins as men and a Life Brand vitamin pill as a puck, recreates NHL hockey games. But it's more complicated than that. He doesn't just do the odd game. He begins playing in September and plays three games a night until spring, when he moves into the playoff rounds. From September through April he actually recreates the entire NHL season in miniature. Though he faithfully replays every game, the results at Zanzibar Gardens are different from the NHL. Michael says he never knows who is going to win a game when it begins. He does all this alone in his apartment at night. At playoff time, however, he gets help from his friends, who come to watch and cheer and provide realistic sound effects.

So it was playoff time and, as I said, there were about

twenty people shoehorned into Michael's dining-room the night I arrived. The first one I was introduced to was Mick O'Connor. By day Mick is a receiver at a Beaver Lumber outlet, but at Zanzibar Gardens he is the PA announcer. With only fifteen minutes to go before game time, Mick wanted to fill me in on what to expect.

"OK. This series is tied two games apiece. It's the Habs against Minnesota and tonight's game is in Minnesota, which will give the North Stars a bit of an edge. Looking around, I'd say we're confident we're going to have a lot of people watching tonight. We're just setting up now for the pre-game, and then we'll set up for the game itself. I think it's going to be an exciting match-up."

It is hard to convey on the printed page what it was like that night at Zanzibar Gardens. Well-known Canadian musician Scott Merritt was huddled over an eight-channel mixer in one corner of the room. He was hovering over wires and dials and speakers and something called a digital reverb. With all this electronic gimmickry, he managed to make the dining-room sound exactly like Maple Leaf Gardens. The room echoed with whistles and horns and the hollow thump of hockey pucks colliding with wood. Opposite Scott in another corner, Ed Roth flicked on a synthesizer. He smiled as it started to hum.

"I'm the organist. I play along with the action and I react as seems fit. It's my job to get the crowd going, so I do things like this . . . (the room reverberates to a familiar rhythmic organ beat). People are supposed to clap with that. It gets the team really worked up and we get much better action. All that regular stuff kind of has to be there or else you just can't have a hockey game."

With moments to go before game time I peered over the arena walls and down at the ice, the way you might watch a cock fight. Suddenly Michael was at my side leading me to what he promised would be a better vantage point. He showed me slots he had cut in the walls of the stands. If I knelt down, he said, I could look through a slot and watch the action from the same perspective I would have if I was actually sitting in the arena. I settled down at a slot in the end Blues and was just getting comfortable when Michael hurried back with a warning.

"The one thing you've got to look out for, as everyone here will tell you, is the puck. It comes up here in the end Blues a lot, and it's really going fast. Now you may think I'm kidding. Hey, guys, I'm telling him about the time there was a girl sitting in the end Blues and I warned her that if she's going to sit there she's going to have to look out for the puck. And she said, 'What? I'm going to have to watch out for this little vitamin tablet flying at me?' Well, it only took a deflection to wing past her ear and hit the window behind her for her to move. The puck really goes quick, so watch out."

At 8 P.M. exactly, the lights in the apartment suddenly went off. It was time for the game to begin. Michael leaned into the arena and snapped on the game lights. Three hooded lamps hung over the ice like lamps in a pool hall. They gave the arena a startlingly realistic glow. On the organist's cue, everyone scrambled to their feet and sang the American and Canadian national anthems. Applause and, yes, catcalls rebounded off the dining-room walls. It all had a magic effect. The lights, the singing, the organ and the sound effects wrapped around the small room and transported us to a fantasy land. The game became inexplicably real. Perhaps that was because every game of hockey we ever see is played in miniature. When we go to the Forum or the Gardens or the Saddledome, the ice always seems small from where we sit. Of course, on television the players are only a few inches high anyway.

As I waited for the game to start, however, I was seized not by philosophic musings on the nature of scale, but by a familiar nervous anticipation that I remembered from sporting events I went to when I was a boy. The feeling was real enough to be almost spooky. Suddenly three things happened at once. Michael slipped into a pair of knee pads, Ed moved to the organ, and Mick picked up his microphone. His voice echoed through the room like he was speaking from high up in the rafters.

"Ladies and gentlemen, welcome to Zanzibar Gardens at Bloomington, Minnesota, for game five of the Stanley Cup finals between the Montreal Canadiens and the Minnesota North Stars."

Over the crowd sound effects, Scott began to play the theme from Hockey Night in Canada on his organ. It sounded remarkably realistic. Mick continued his introductions over the music.

"The referee for tonight's game is Kerry Fraser. The linesmen are Kevin Collins and John D'Amico. . ."

The announcement was Michael's cue to crawl out on his knee pads to centre ice, pushing the hockey coin players in front of him and sounding remarkably like a kid who had heard too much Danny Gallivan.

"And that's the Montreal Canadiens coming out onto the ice ... there's Patrick Roy, of course, Robinson, Chelios, Smith, Gainey and Naslund ... looks like will be the starting line-up. And now the North Stars heading out, led by Don Beaupré. Here come Maruk, McClelland, Bellows, Hartsburg and Brooke."

Finally the game began. Michael, who was still on his knees, began to push the hockey coin players around the rink much the same way a kid might push toy trucks around a sandbox. Except this kid was on speed. He picked up the coins, swiped at the vitamin pill puck, threw the coins down again, and up again, all with the slick confidence of a street hustler playing three-card monte. He passed the puck from coin to coin, stickhandling past opponents and winding up to shoot on net like Boom Boom Geoffrion. Sometimes when he shot, his arm swung around over his head and he hit the vitamin pill so fast that no matter how hard you watched, you couldn't see where it went. Once someone videotaped a game, and even when they slowed the video down they couldn't follow the slap shots.

All the while he was playing, Michael kept up a running commentary in the style of Danny Gallivan. He was good enough at Gallivan's voice that he could have slipped into his announcer's booth twenty years ago and fooled more than me. At the beginning of the second period the score was tied, 2-2.

"We're all set now, referee Kerry Fraser is ready to drop the puck ... and time is in for this the second period. From the face-off it's back into the Montreal end with Robinson, up here to Gainey ... a small collision there ... Robinson back to Chelios, here's a chance, Gainey on the wing ... a long shot, here comes Robinson with the rebound – HE SCORES, wait now – no . . . there it is, the light's on. A little delay there, we weren't sure; a second before the light came on. We'll wait and get the official response on that goal."

That, of course, was Mick O'Connor's cue. Remember Mick? He's the rink announcer.

"Montreal goal scored by number 19 Larry Robinson . . . assisted by 23 Bob Gainey, at 45 seconds."

The crowd, which seemed to be partial to the Canadiens that night, cheered and yelled and actually threw things on the ice. The little plastic things that you use to do up loaves of bread seemed, for some reason, to be the favoured projectile. Later in the second period, Roberts checked Nyland in the corner and there was nearly a fight. Play stopped as the coins milled around; I was seized by the urge to return some night with a tiny plastic octopus or a dead guppy to fling onto the ice.

There was also an injury. Which is what happens when a player's coin gets bumped and lands face down, or when someone's picture pops out of its plastic frame.

Between periods the die-hard fans stayed in the living-room and watched Michael carefully apply a coat of spray Pledge wax to the ice surface. Most of us, however, retired to the kitchen to eat the hot dogs that had been boiling in a big pot on the stove. That was where I met Michael's girlfriend.

Judy Hall is a telephone operator. As we talked I couldn't help thinking that to get to the playoffs Michael had played out a 500-plus game season. Since September he had averaged over three games of hockey a night. I asked Judy what happened on a typical league night in Zanzibar Gardens.

"Normally he plays in the dining-room by himself, and he'll have the arena lights on, and all the other lights will be off, just like tonight. I'm usually in the living-room or the bedroom. And usually he talks really low, and all of a sudden I hear him say, SCORE! But he likes to play by himself and I usually leave him alone."

"Do you guys have fights about it?" I wonder.

"Ah, yes," she says. "I think he spends too much time at it. I want to do other things. He just gets so involved. Sometimes I can hardly wait for the season to end."

The season wasn't over, but the game soon was. Montreal beat Minnesota 7-6. Robinson got the winning goal at the two-minute mark of the overtime period. While everyone else talked excitedly about the winning goal, I took Michael into his bedroom and we sat on the bed away from everyone else and talked for a few minutes about Zanzibar Gardens. He told me that he and Mick invented the game when they were kids. They did it because they wanted to do something different than just play table hockey. The game, in a much simpler incarnation, was stored for years in Michael's parents' garage. He dug it out six years ago and began to play again as a diversion.

Playing, says Michael, who is a songwriter, has helped him with his writing. It relaxes him, he says. The thing he likes the best is when teams play on the west coast.

"Some of the best games are those late ones. I play them at their time. Like at eleven o'clock at night or whatever it would be. There is a great mood to those games, a great atmosphere. Of course, I change the lighting for all the arenas. They have dimmer lighting out west. It's more of a yellow light than a white light.

Rather than that overhead type of factory light, it's more atmospheric. Sometimes it's really great because there'll be a tip-in, a shot that happens one in a thousand times, where it's tipped or rebounds in, or it's deflected. That's magic. That's when you wish you had a camera or somebody could see it. You have to see it to believe it, it's as simple as that."

And that, I suppose, is the ultimate truth about Zanzibar Gardens. You do have to see it to believe it.

We had hardly begun talking when someone knocked on the bedroom door and said we had to come back to the arena. There was something important left to do. We went back to the dining-room where everyone was waiting. As soon as we arrived, Michael dropped to his knees and nodded at Mick. Mick brought the microphone up to his mouth and the organ started up as Mick began a familiar announcement.

"Ladies and gentlemen, the three star selection as selected by Hockey Night in Canada. The first star, from the Montreal Canadiens, number 19, Larry Robinson. The second star, from the North Stars, with three goals, number 4, Craig Hartsburg. And the third star from tonight's game, from the Montreal Canadiens, with two goals, number 21, Kjell Dahlin."

As Mick called each player's name, Michael rolled the appropriate coin out onto the ice of Zanzibar Gardens. Everyone applauded the choices. As we clapped, the coins rolled out from Michael's hand towards the palm tree insignia that graced centre ice. Then, as if by magic, each coin described a smooth circle and rolled right back to Michael. I looked down at him in disbelief. He smiled back at me and winked.

HIGH ANXIETY

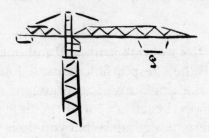

A few years ago I spent an unfortunate day on a
construction site. I had gone with the intention of
talking to everyone who worked there. Unfortunately, it didn't take long to learn that, these days, cranes are
the heart of any construction site. I am talking about the
big ones that you see suspended high over modern
buildings. The ones that kind of wave in the wind like
wonky giraffe necks made of steel. Unfortunately, it was
going to be difficult to ignore the crane. Not that I am
afraid of heights or anything.

You see, once a building gets going, nothing can
happen without the crane. The carpenters need it to
deliver their wood. The electricians need it to lift their
supplies to them. The cement trucks need it to haul their
cement off the street and onto the building. Once things
start humming, the different trades usually spend a good
part of each day fighting for crane time. The crane is
always at the centre of things. Which is, unfortunately,
where I was supposed to be.

I set off to investigate the world of the construction

39

crane in a good humour. It never occurred to me that anyone would try to get me into one.

My first surprise was that it actually takes two guys to operate each crane. There is the driver inside the crane with his hands on the controls, and there is a guy on the ground called the swamper. Larry was the swamper on the job I visited.

"A swamper's job is to look after the crane from the ground. He has to hook it up and unhook it, and if anything falls, he's responsible because he is responsible for all the hook-ups. The swamper also has to guide the driver, because a lot of the time the driver can't see where he's going. What you do is guide him with your hands – your thumbs, really – in and out. It's called a trolley: trolley in and trolley out. Sometimes we use the radio, but we try to avoid using the radio as much as possible, because there are people using the radio who need it more than we do, like for an emergency. So you try to stay off the radio."

Larry and I were standing on the edge of a shaft in a corner of the construction site. We were waiting for Larry's crane to deliver a bucket full of gravel. Larry suddenly interrupted himself. I looked up and saw the bucket swinging against the blue sky and heading towards us like a gigantic cannon-ball. I took an involuntary step backward. Larry raised a thumb and reached out unconsciously as if he could actually catch the bucket.

"Here he comes now, he's going to drop the gravel down the shaft, which is, what would you say, fifteen feet or so wide. I'm just going to open the bucket, and we're going to drop the stones three floors down. He's not going to be able to see us down here so he's got to be careful, very careful. You get used to a crane operator, you know? You can just look up at him and he knows what you mean. But he can't see anything, and with one slip I could lose my job. I've got to be very careful. My worst nightmare is having something fall on someone's head, I guess. That's my nightmare. I would never want to see that. I'd never want to see it, never. It's never happened to me. But believe me, it does happen."

Larry and I stood on the edge of the shaft for about an hour, he talking and me silently marvelling at the skill of the man whose hands were on the controls nine storeys above us. He couldn't see us clearly because our shaft was tucked away behind a wall, yet he set load after load down at our feet as delicately and as elegantly as if the bucket were full of eggs rather than gravel. It was a feat that called for more than a little trust between the swamper and the crane operator.

Later in the day over coffee, I was introduced to another swamper. His name was Tony, and when someone told him I was a journalist, he wanted to tell me about the trust that must exist between the driver and the swamper.

"If the driver doesn't trust you, you cannot work together. You've got to trust him and he's got to trust you. You've got to work together and trust each other. Sometimes it's dangerous, but if you know what you're doing it's never too dangerous. It's part of the job. It's construction. Sometimes things happen."

After coffee I watched Tony work the concrete bucket. He stood on the street beside an ever-changing parade of cement trucks and gestured to Wally, his operator, in a sequence of signals that would do a third-base coach proud. The bucket would swoop out of the sky like a 747 and then stop dead and float magically about two inches off the ground. They did this all afternoon. I kept waiting for a mistake, for the moment the bucket would bite into the asphalt or thump into a cement truck. It never happened.

A lot of people on construction sites think the men who drive the cranes are crazy. Maybe. You'd have to be crazy to do that job, they say. Well, yes. To crawl into their cranes at least. Have you ever wondered how they get up there?

I always thought there was an elevator running up the middle of the crane. There isn't. It turns out the drivers climb hand over hand up the crane. And as likely as not they climb up there at seven-thirty in the morning and don't come down all day. They don't have time for a lunch break or a coffee break, because if they stop the whole site has to grind to a halt. They take a plastic bottle up and use it if they need to go to the toilet.

The only thing that'll get them out of their gondola early is wind. If the wind starts to blow, they come down pretty quickly. Or so Alex told me. Alex drove one of the cranes on the site I was visiting.

"Arguments always happen when the boss says it's not too windy, and I say it is. I will not jeopardize my licence or my job and kill somebody, just because the boss says it's OK. Like it happened to me on one job. I came down and I said I'm not going to work anymore, that's it, and he says there's no wind. And I said there's no wind down here but you go up there. He told me there's no way you're going home, and I told him that I've locked up the crane and nobody is going to touch it. So he went up, and when he came down he said, it's OK, I understand. But he knows if I refuse there is nothing he can do about it. He cannot push me into some kind of accident, because if some kind of accident happens, the judge won't go to him, he'll come to me."

Alex has operated cranes on some of the tallest construction sites in the country. He was an operator on the TD Centre, for instance, which means he has sat in cranes that were higher than the tallest building in Canada. He said the most difficult thing about working on skyscrapers is that you can't see the load you are hoisting.

He said his worst moment on the job happened when he was hauling a load to the roof of the TD Centre.

"The wind all of a sudden just came up. It just picked up the load. Just grabbed it and took it away. I couldn't hold it with the brake anymore. I figured it's going to go right into the Royal Bank across the road. So I had to stop hoisting the load. I just played with the boom, up and down, to take the swing out. I watched the cable because you can't see nothing. Everybody ran away, because the wind was so high. That was the most scary thing I ever did. Finally I swung to the other side of the building. I made it in between the two buildings, and I sat there for five minutes. I really didn't believe that I'd made it. The guys I spoke to on the telephone said they figured the load was gone. They figured it was going to go right in, and I was going with it."

Of course I knew I should climb the crane and get into the gondola with Wally. And of course when I finally started up, I turned on my tape recorder and registered the entire sorry adventure for posterity. Why I didn't take my cue from American president Richard Nixon and just erase the moment is beyond me. I didn't. And since I have already humiliated myself on national radio, there doesn't seem to be any good reason for holding anything back in this book. I am about to reproduce here, for your merriment and my shame, what transpired the afternoon I attempted to scale the side of Wally's crane. But first I want you to imagine a three-storey house. Now picture another three-storey house perched on top of that one. Now put a third one on top of the second one. You should be looking at three houses piled on top of each other. In order to join Wally, I had to climb to the roof of the third house. I was standing at the bottom of the first ladder when I turned my machine on. I will admit to being somewhat nervous.

> "Test, one, two, three. I'm standing in the middle of the . . . let's get a grip on myself here. I'm standing in the middle of the . . . I'm standing in the middle of the shaft of the crane, in the section that will become the elevator shaft. I'm holding onto the ladder with one foot on the ground and one foot on the first rung of the ladder. Oh, my God, the damn thing is swinging. I mean, the whole shaft, the whole crane, all twenty-six tonnes of it is swinging . . . it's moving an inch back and forth. It's not steady. This . . . oh, God, here he comes now. The guy is coming up to make me climb."

The guy who was coming to make me climb was Alex, the crane operator I had spoken to earlier. He had prepared me in the office only moments before.

"No problem, Stuart," he kept on saying. "Just don't look down. Look straight ahead and keep climbing."

I thought it would be too humiliating to have him find me frozen at the foot of the crane so, biting down on my tongue, I pulled myself onto the first rung and began my journey. I made it up the first ladder to a sort of landing. I had, essentially, made it to the roof of the first house.

Almost. In order to get to the second ladder I had to step onto the landing and walk about five feet.

No matter how hard I tried, I couldn't make myself let go of my ladder. I was clutching it for dear life. I tried to tell myself that this was silly, I could do it. Meanwhile every sensible cell in my body urged me to get down. My body parts won. Although I felt ashamed, I also felt relief. Imagine what it would have been like higher up. I climbed down. Alex was standing at the bottom, grinning.

"So, tell me, how did it feel, up one floor?" he asked.

"I was scared," I replied bravely.

"Well, it doesn't even move where you were," he said smugly. "Just a little bit."

"It was moving back and forth about an inch," I yelped, "and I was scared."

"An inch is nothing, absolutely nothing. You should have gone up all the way."

"How much is it moving at the top?" I wondered aloud.

"Oh, I would say about six inches."

"Back and forth?"

"Yes. Watch the tower every time he picks up the bucket. Watch the way it moves. Compare it to the other buildings. You see how it's going back and forth."

"Holy crow."

"Up there it's even worse, but it's something you have to get used to. You've got to have a good stomach."

The next time you look at one of these cranes, line it up against something that doesn't move, like a building. Line it up and watch how it swings. They make them out of soft steel on purpose so they will sway like that instead of snapping under the pressure of a heavy load. The concept of the crane snapping with me clutching it halfway up is something that I hadn't, until Alex mentioned it, considered. I felt I had gone far enough. No sense taking any foolish risks.

I went home defeated, but accepting my lot in life as a coward. Some men are meant to climb cranes. Some aren't.

I came back the next day determined to do better.

I made it up the first level of the ladder somewhat more easily. Then I let go of the ladder and, imbued with courage, actually crawled across the platform towards the bottom of the second ladder. Halfway across the platform I decided I should turn on the tape recorder and say something. As you read this I want you to imagine me huddled a third of the way up the crane. I am clutching a steel girder for all I am worth. If I had had 1,000 arms, 999 of them would have been clinging to the structure. I would have used one to cautiously turn my machine on.

"[Gravely] I have climbed the first level. And I'm now on a sort of landing. What I haven't done is look down [with growing concern]. I'm sitting on this metal grate, so that underneath me . . . oh, God, it's shaking [getting a grip]. It's like standing on a grate in a sidewalk so you can see down through it. And what I haven't done is look down to see what it looks like beneath me, and I'm going to do that now; [in complete control] all I'm trying to do is get the courage to look down. I'm sitting rather than standing, and holding on for dear life to this ladder, this piece of steel. I'm going to look directly down [I seem to be losing it here]. It's six floors down underneath me, and I'm terrified. I'm going to look down [surprise] . . . oh, that's not so bad [oops] . . .

whoa, it's not that great, either. It's sort of swinging up here – oh, God! OK, hold on, ha-ha, it just got a bit, a little woozy there. This whole thing seems to be swinging a bit and I think I have gone far enough. I think I'm going to put the tape recorder away now. You'll forgive me if I call it quits here on the sixth floor."

I didn't even consider going higher. Or, actually, I did. And all I could think of was freezing mid-way between platforms. What would happen, I wondered, if I got halfway between levels and just froze. Would someone come and talk me down? Or worse, up? I had a vision of the TV networks coming to shoot pictures of me clutching the "ladder of death." And I kept remembering Alex's command not to look down. Why not? What would happen? Could a peek to the ground be so horrible that my hands might fly off the ladder in an involuntary motion of horror? What would happen then? Would I balance on my feet, or plunge immediately to an unspeakable death? Why was I there, anyway? What a stupid thing to try to do. To climb a nine-storey ladder. Who did I think I was, anyway? God, I was going to die.

When I got to the bottom, Larry the swamper was waiting for me.

"You're not going to go up in the crane, or what?" he asked. I didn't say anything.

"You're not going to go up?" he repeated.

"It's not that I'm . . . uh . . . I didn't go very high, did I?" I said, staring at the ground.

"No, you went about maybe twenty-five feet and looked around and that's it. Climb up all the way. I'll climb up with you," he offered.

"I just don't think I can do it," I said gravely. "It is

kind of you to offer. But I just don't think I can do
it."

Larry was holding a radio, which suddenly barked to
life.

"Wally wants to talk to you," he said, pointing to the
top of the crane I had failed to scale.

I looked up. Wally the crane operator had emerged
from his gondola and was, my God, he was dancing, doing
a jig on the boom of the crane. I felt my knees go loose.
He was talking into his walkie-talkie as he danced nine
storeys above the ground.

"If you want to be a crane operator, you've got to
have a little bit of guts and get up in the air. It helps
to be crazy up here. Why don't you join me?"

I wish I could, Wally. I really do.

FLAGS UNLIMITED

Gordon Burke loved flags.

And you would have thought that 1967 would have been a shrewd year to open a flag store in Canada. Lester Pearson was prime minister, the centennial summer was just over the horizon, and the new Canadian flag was, or should have been, on everyone's shopping list. The trouble was, there just weren't that many people with shopping lists in Thornton, Ontario.

In 1966 Thornton, Ontario, was still a village of two hundred people ripped right out of the pages of a Stephen Leacock short story. On the main street there was Jim Rainey the blacksmith, Vernon Jennet the barber, the general store, the volunteer fire department, of course, and even the creek at the edge of town. In those days, when it was winter, there was also snow. Real snow. Snow that floated down out of the night and piled up to almost the roof by winter's end.

It was snowing like that the night Gordon Burke moved his family to Thornton. They struggled through the snow into their new apartment on top of the storefront on the main street. Gordon was actually moving to Thornton so he could open an upholstery business, which is how his father and his grandfather had made their living. But when he finally got around to it, he hung two shingles outside the new store. One said "Gordon Burke Upholstery". The other said "Flags Unlimited". As I have already mentioned, Gordon loved flags.

Gordon wasn't really expecting to sell that many flags to his new neighbours in Thornton. What he was counting on was attracting some of the steady stream of families that drove through Thornton on their way to cottage country in the north.

The trouble was, as Gordon's son Ed remembers, that instead of dropping in to buy the new flag, people were lining up to complain about it.

> "Dad heard the complaints from everyone. They were buying anything but the Canadian flag. They'd come in and ask for the Ontario flag or the Red Ensign or even the Union Jack. He kept saying, 'We've got our new national flag, why aren't you buying it?' and people would tell him, 'because it fades.' They called it the Pearson pennant, and he used to think it was sad nobody would put the new flag up. The reason being that it always seemed to turn pink on people. So he said we had to come up with a better flag. So we started sewing flags instead of printing them."

Before Gordon Burke started sewing flags, nearly every flag that was manufactured in Canada was printed. They were made much the way T-shirts are made today. Manufacturers would take a piece of white cloth and print the red maple leaf and the red bars in place. This looked fine in the store window, but after a few months on a pole at someone's cottage, the red ink invariably ran, leaving a lot of pink flags that looked a lot like faded T-shirts flapping in the wind. Instead of printing his flags, Gordon began sewing pieces of red material and white material together piece by piece. If you wanted a good Canadian flag in 1967, you had to go to Gordon the upholsterer on the main street of Thornton, Ontario.

Unfortunately, Gordon wasn't exactly swamped with orders – neither for flags nor for his services as an upholsterer. Money was tight and it became even tighter when an uncle and aunt died and the Burkes found themselves with three extra children. The growing family was squeezed into the upstairs of the store. The four boys shared one small bedroom; the girls another. At exam time some of the kids used to retreat to closets in search of a quiet corner where they could study. Times were lean, and Gordon's wife, Beth, remembers wondering if they were going to squeak through.

"I think the worst moment was just after we obtained the three extra children. That meant we had eight, and there were quite a few of them to be made ready for high school. I remember that September. I'd say it was a day or two before school was to open, and I was wondering how I was going to dress these kids and get them off to school properly. Well, it had happened that the lady next door had passed away and they were having a very large auction sale. A gentleman came in, and it was raining very heavily, and he said to me, 'What's wrong with you people; why aren't you doing something to feed these people at this auction sale? They don't want to leave, but they are starving.' So I looked at Gordon and he looked at me. We had been planning for school, of course, as far as food was concerned. We had a freezer full of sandwiches for the children's lunches. There was over a week's worth of sandwiches there,

so we decided, OK, and pulled all the frozen sandwiches out of the freezer and sold every one of them.
I think we collected $63. I outfitted all the kids with
that $63 and started them off for school.''

Eventually, to make ends meet, Gordon took on a couple
of part-time jobs. First he became the caretaker of the
Thornton Arena. Later he added school bus driver to his
string of occupations. He juggled the jobs like a plate
spinner working a small town convention. He'd leave the
house at six and hustle over to flood the rink before
breakfast. He'd get home from the rink just in time to
drive the school bus at eight. During the day he'd work in
the upholstery shop or turn out a few flags. In the
afternoon he'd drive the bus again. At night he'd close up
the arena.

The kids had things on the go as well. In the summer
they sold worms to fishermen and ice to tourists. Every
night fifty-five trays of water went into the freezer. Every
morning the ice was bagged and readied for the passing
trade. Sometimes when tourists were poking around in
the freezer looking for ice, they would come up holding
some of the family's groceries. Beth would sell anything if
she could turn a profit.

Then with the downstairs completely overrun by over-
stuffed chesterfields and half-sewn flags, Gordon and
Beth converted their upstairs living-room into a dance
studio and offered dance lessons to people in Thornton.
Gordon had been a professional dancer before he
married.

What with the arena, the bus, the flags, the upholstery
and the dancing, Gordon didn't have a lot of free time.
But his daughter Val remembers he still found time for
her.

"He would wake me up at three o'clock in the morning to watch Fred Astaire movies. My dad was very, very sensitive to his children. He knew we all had individual needs. I'd learned how to dance with my father, and he would watch the TV Guide to see if there was a Fred Astaire movie coming on. And if there was, he would wake me up at three o'clock in the morning, school day or not. I remember him whispering, 'Val, wake up, there's a Fred Astaire movie on.' He would set the alarm for this and we would sit there and cry and watch Fred Astaire together, because we used to love to watch him tap dance all the time. That's the type of guy he was. He loved to make people happy. It was his prime concern."

There is a thing they do in those Fred Astaire movies when they want to show the passage of time. They take a calendar and superimpose it on a scene, and then they start flipping the pages of the calendar one after another. I am going to start flipping pages here.

So imagine a white clapboard storefront on the main street of Thornton. A page flips and Gordon is sewing a flag on an old Singer sewing machine; a page flips and Gordon is driving the school bus; another page and he is hauling the water barrel around the arena to freeze the rink; another page and there are three more kids in his family; another page and Auntie Bea has moved to Thornton and has added her handmade oven mitts to the store downstairs; another page and they are dancing upstairs; another page and someone walks into the store, looks at the oven mitts, the couches and the flags, scratches her head and walks out again. The last page of the calendar says 1980, and damned if the couches haven't been pushed to the back of the store and the flags moved up front and aren't orders coming in and going out and Gordon has hired a few of the local women to help him cut and sew and he is not the biggest flag manufacturer in the country but he is big enough to have employees and customers and things are looking up for the first time in a long time – which, of course, is when Gordon dies. Dancing. Drops dead on the dance floor. Heart attack. It is 1983. He is fifty-two years old. His son Ed was barely twenty.

> "When Dad died, a lot of our competitors thought, there goes Flags Unlimited. I think they kind of thought the place was going to fall apart. I think there was even a few attempts to see if we would be willing to sell, but we knew that wouldn't have been something Dad would have liked."

In 1984 Beth and the kids decided to keep the flag business going. Two events converged to prove that this was a wise decision. First, retailers began to see flags as a cheap and effective way of drawing attention to their stores. McDonald's led the way. A lot of people followed. Second, the Pope came to Canada. One morning Beth and the kids woke up and found themselves looking at an order for one million pocket-sized Canadian flags. Flags for Canadians to wave at the Pope. They took the order and filled it and things haven't been the same since. By the summer of 1985, there were fifteen people making flags in the upholstery store on the main street of Thornton. Things were a little crowded. The three-person art department worked out of the basement and had to struggle into rubber boots every time it rained. Upstairs, things were no better. There were six people working at a cutting table designed for one. Sometimes a seventh person would arrive with a rush order, and the six would scoop their work off the table and hold it in the air while

the seventh cut something quickly. When she was finished, the original six would lay their material down and
go back to work. The Burkes were still living upstairs.
Flags Unlimited was a significant little enterprise being
run out of someone's house. It was the ultimate cottage
industry. The office staff was crammed into a miniature
room off the kitchen. Valerie Tonna was the office
manager.

"There were three of us basically that worked in
there full time. And if a fourth person came in you
couldn't swing a cat around. That's how close the
shipping desks were. You literally climbed over
things to get into files or get outdoors. Phones were
passed from one to the other. It was comical because
there was only one phone between two desks. If you
wanted to use the phone you had to wait your turn
and climb over boxes and things to get to it. It was
like a Marx Brothers movie. Total confusion at times,
but it was fun, it was, it was fun. It was like no other
business I'd ever worked for or known."

In September 1985, Flags Unlimited officially opened
their new 11,000-square-foot factory warehouse just off
Highway 400 near Barrie. In case you can't visualize it,
11,000 square feet is a lot of factory. Gordon's widow,
Beth, oversaw the opening ceremonies as president. And
when they opened for business the next day, six of the
eight kids were working there full time. Some of them
were in the offices, some of them were on sewing
machines and some of them were in the shipping room.
Paul, the eldest son, assumed the responsibilities of
executive vice-president. His business plan that year
called for Flags Unlimited to do over a million dollars in
sales. They made it. By the time I visited, they had
thirty-three employees and were figuring on fifty a year

down the road. They had a time clock, a front office and a lunch room. As Val and I walked around the plant, she pointed people out to me. "That lady used to babysit me," she said. "I changed that girl's diapers when she was young." We passed a blackboard in the print room. It had the next day's orders written in blue chalk. "Island of St. Vincent," it said, "5,000 flags, 4 x 6'." Under that, "Village of Ailsa Craig, Ontario, 12 flags." Flags Unlimited is now the third-biggest flag manufacturer in the country and growing.

Everyone had gone home. Val and I were alone in the plant.

"I'm going to lock up," she said. "Want to help me take the flags down?"

We went out to the parking lot and began to pull down the three flags flapping in the evening breeze.

"Be careful," she said, "not to let the flag touch the ground."

"Why not?" I asked.

"I'm not sure," she replied, clutching two of the flags carefully off the ground. "Dad taught me that. You're never supposed to let a flag touch the ground."

We carried the flags back into the plant and I said my goodbyes. As I pulled out of the parking lot, Val stood in the doorway of the new building, waving. I waved back and wondered what Gordon Burke would think if he knew what had happened to his family. As I spun along the highway towards the city, I also wondered if there are any fathers left who would wake their daughters up at three in the morning so they could watch a Fred Astaire movie together.

Maybe. But I don't know them.

THE ART OF
SHOVELLING SNOW

When I was a boy, I became convinced that the force that propelled my mother through each day was her belief that if she and the Queen ever met, they would become best friends. Mother believed, I thought, that what Her Majesty really wanted more than anything – more than charades at Balmoral, more than Welsh corgis on the moors, more than folk dances in Bali – was a cup of tea and a chat at our kitchen table. I settled on this notion as the only logical explanation as to why Mom was so concerned about the state of my room and my manners. It seemed to me, at the time, that you would only worry about those things if you feared the Queen herself might drop by at any moment.

It was her fantasy, not mine. More correctly, I suppose, it was my fantasy about her fantasy. Whatever. Ever since I was a teenager, whenever I face a driveway full of snow, I become my mother's son. Every drift I dig into, each bank I bear down on, I do for Her Majesty. I shovel with the certain knowledge that soon the Queen will arrive. And I shovel knowing that before she comes, a member of the royal staff will be dispatched to examine my work, to see if it is up to snuff. That is why I fuss over the edges of the banks, the angles, the smoothness, the evenness under foot. And that is why, when I have finished, I stand and survey my work with such pleasure. For me and my walk, both the form and the function of the job are important. Because they would both be important to Her Majesty.

Perhaps this is why I have always found shovelling snow the most satisfying work, and feel sorry for people who live in parts of this country where it is not possible to add it to the list of chores.

I remember with great affection the driveway of my childhood. It was long and narrow, like a canyon wedged between two houses. At one end was the garage, against which we played ball hockey. In those days we only played when there was snow to shovel. And we tended the surface of the driveway with the care a greenskeeper gives a championship golf course. The trick was to expose enough asphalt for traction and still leave enough snow for slidability. We strove for a sort of mottled effect – patches of snow and patches of pavement – and if we did our job properly, when we finished, the driveway looked like the side of a fine Holstein.

There was no salt in those days, of course. I think salt has soured the season. Now that we can get rid of snow, rather than just pile it up, we have come to resent it whenever it lingers. In those days there was only sand, and even the city wouldn't scrape through to the bare concrete of a winter sidewalk. Like us, they left a layer of packed snow that sealed the sidewalk until spring. They sent a sand wagon after the plough. We all envied the man who rode the sand wagon. He rode it the way you would ride a dogsled. His job was to control the rate at which the sand poured out of the wagon. It was the kind of job you wanted when you grew up. The sand looked like cinnamon on the snow, and you don't see that anymore. In the spring, water pooled in the sand like it might pool on a beach in the Spice Islands, and little boys would build dams and work the sand like engineers. Supervising the sand was a rite of spring. It took hours and days for my friends and me to ready the sidewalk for summer. If they could, men from the city came and collected the sand and, unbelievably, used it again the next winter.

Of course, we didn't limit our shovelling to our own driveways. We shouldered our shovels and marched from door to door, turning our passions into profit. It is a curious business, shovelling walks for money. There are unspoken conventions that all boys know and follow. A boy never, for instance, does walks in his immediate neighbourhood. You will not often know the boy who comes to your front door on a snowy evening with a shovel tucked under his arm. He always comes from a few streets over. Your child, or your neighbour's child, always goes, through some soft understanding, and knocks on doors a few streets over. It is somehow not proper to ask someone you know for money to clear snow. That's another thing. Price is never discussed in advance. Shovelling snow is like practising law or dentistry. It is a job where manners matter, where money isn't mentioned. When the job is done, one presents one's bill by presenting oneself and announcing simply, "I am finished." It's the homeowner who must wrestle with what would be too little and what would be too much money for the job.

When you're shovelling for money, driveways are seldom done. It is the economy of scale. The bang per buck just isn't there. You usually get paid more than it is worth to do a walk. Always less than it is worth to do the drive. So no one does them. The only people who do driveways are the real professionals who drive vehicles or push mechanical devices and charge professional rates. Or people like me, the shovel people, who actually like it.

Somewhere around puberty it becomes not OK to go out shovelling snow for money. It is like Hallowe'en. There comes a time when you can't go door to door anymore. This is a problem for people who actually like shovelling, because it restricts the amount of shovelling they can get in. Shovelling, you see, is not like jogging. I have heard that joggers can experience what is known as a "jogger's high". When that happens they can always extend their run and stay high. A shoveller does not have the same luxury.

I have done most of my shovelling at night. Dug into drifts and chipped at ice under the stars. And when I have finished I have stood at the edge of my property and coveted the snow on my neighbour's walk. Once you have swung down your walk, what else can you do? You can work your way back and widen it a bit. Or you can square up the edges. But if you are really going, if you are on a "shoveller's high", you need deep snow. And there, in front of you, lies your neighbour's walk. Untouched. The dilemma is that people just don't do that sort of thing today. What would you say to your neighbour if you came face to face? What would the neighbourhood say about you behind closed doors if, after every snowfall, you swung up and down both sides of the street and shovelled all the walks? At best you would be resented. So those of us who love to shovel don't get enough time in, and that is why we are out there so fast when it is really snowing. And that is why we take such pains to do the job right.

As to the question of tools, I am a purist. There are the ploughs that you push, and they are all right after a light dusting; in fact, they are quite efficient on a driveway after a light snowfall, and are probably the closest I will ever come to driving heavy equipment. The best shovels, however, are the kind you can swing like an axe. A shovel that bites into the bank. A shovel that allows you to flip your snow into a pile. Best of all, however, are shovels made from wood. You can't buy wooden shovels anymore, but there is a woman in Montreal West who knows how I feel about these things, and she wrote to me recently and promised to leave me her wooden shovel in her will. I am happy to wait. In the meantime I make do with what I have and watch the weather from November to March. Waiting for snow. And my moments of royal glory.

THE COLDWATER PHONE COMPANY

I fell in love with Coldwater, Ontario, after I spent a day at their annual fall fair. I went to the fair quite by accident. We (we being my producer and I) decided it would be fun to visit a fair for"Morningside". My wife, Linda, suggested I try Coldwater.

"Where?" I asked.

"It's this lovely little town I saw last weekend," she replied. "I stopped there for a sandwich because I loved the name."

"That's not the way journalists work," I explained patiently.

I called the Ontario agriculture information department.

"I was wondering," I asked, "if you could tell me where I might find a good country fair this weekend? I want a real authentic sort of folksy fair, if you know what I mean."

There was a pause while the man from the agriculture department flipped through his list of fairs.

"How about Coldwater?" he said.

It was about a year later that Linda brought up Coldwater again.

"You should do something about the Coldwater Phone Company," she said.

"What's so special about it?" I asked.

"Phone and find out," she said.

I didn't know there were communities in Canada that owned their own phone systems. I had always been under the impression that Bell Canada had the whole country sewn up. But there are, it turns out, pockets of independence from coast to coast. Edmonton owns its own phone company. So does Thunder Bay. And so, it turns out, does Coldwater, Ontario.

The Coldwater Municipal Phone Company could be the smallest phone company in Canada. It has four employees and 880 paying customers. Small enough so that as recently as 1984, company employees still hand-wrote the monthly bills that were sent out to each house in town.

"Coldwater," said someone, "has everything." And maybe they are right. There's a river that sort of meanders through the centre of town, and a doctor who still does house calls, and railroad tracks, and a feed mill, a great fall fair, a war memorial and now, I find out, a phone company with a history worth telling.

It wasn't always so.

In fact, what makes this story so inspirational is that Bell Canada was in Coldwater first. As Ian Murray, the present manager of the Coldwater Municipal Phone Company, tells it, Bell once owned all the telephones in town. But when Bell, as is Bell's wont, tried to raise the monthly rates, everyone in town got stirred up, so they held a meeting where they decided to buy Bell out. That was in 1916.

"Bell had about fourteen customers in town at the time and had decided on raising the rates, and there were strong feelings in town that Bell was going to be charging too much. People figured they could run the phones more economically than Bell Canada, and they agreed to purchase the whole system, lock, stock and barrel. What they did was they got together and formed a municipal system, as it was known then and is still known now, which consisted of a hundred people putting up their homes as collateral for the purchase of the company. They took out a debenture, borrowed the money from the banks and ended up owning the company, with a hundred people having a share in it.''

Maybe that sort of thing could only have happened in 1916. The notion of finding one hundred people prepared to mortgage their homes today because their phone bill was getting out of line boggles the mind. And while it is one thing to start something like that, it is another kettle of fish to keep it going. Especially for seventy-five years. In baseball you would call that going into extra innings. Baseball teams have relief pitchers to call on when things get tight. Coldwater had the town druggist, Mord Millard.

They just don't make people like Mr Millard anymore. In the back of his drugstore he ran an insurance agency, and between prescriptions he would skip to the back and write insurance policies. He was also a notary public and did everyone's wills. For good measure he repaired clocks on the side. So in 1916, when his friends and neighbours bought out Bell Canada, they turned to Mr Millard for help and (are you surprised?), on top of everything else, he soon became Coldwater's Mr Telephone. He strung all the lines in town. Alone. Unless it involved putting up a new pole. He'd hire extra help if he had to put up a pole. But if a line came down in the rain, it was Mr Millard who struggled into his raincoat and slogged out to fix it. He had no training in electronics whatsoever, yet over the years he basically built the entire Coldwater phone system singlehandedly. And, says Ian Murray, who has to repair it today, he did it his way.

> "There's one circuit in the back that's still in opera-
> tion today, that was designed and built by Mr Millard.
> It's the one that controls the fire siren for the
> volunteer fire department in town. I know it's his
> work. It has his personal touch all over it. Like to
> protect it from dust and that, he encased it in a
> medicine bottle. It's definitely his handiwork. Some-
> times when I am working on wiring jobs I open up
> some nightmares back there. But that's what happens
> when you get someone designing a one-of-a-kind
> system. When repair time comes around and that
> gentleman has passed along, he's taken all the infor-
> mation with him. So sometimes you start a circuit
> Mr Millard built and you realize it's a one-of-a-kind
> and there is no information around on it. You know
> you're in for a couple of days' work just to figure it
> out before you can start to repair it."

Ian Murray and I were sitting over a coffee in the lunch-room of the Coldwater Municipal Phone Company. He had his feet propped up on the table and seemed to be enjoying his reminiscing.

Suddenly he swung his legs down and leaned forward.

"What we should do," he said, "is invite a few people over."

So we did.

And I sat there in the lunch-room for the rest of the afternoon while a steady stream of townsfolk marched in to talk to me about their telephones.

The first was Gladdy. Now retired, she once worked for Mr Millard himself. Gladdy was an operator. Back before

automatic dialling came in. Back when people would pick
their telephones off the wall and say, "Gladdy, give me
Charlie at the hardware, will you?"

I only had one question for Gladdy. I wanted to
know whether she would admit to listening in on
conversations.

"Oh, sure. All the time, especially on the rural lines
because everybody was on the rural lines. There
would be twenty, maybe thirty people on the line at
once, so what difference did it make if the operator
came on? I remember I had one customer – and he
was a crusty old fellow – he had some money and he
thought he owned the telephone. Well, his line would
be busy with folks just talking generalities about what
they were doing, and he would come on and say, 'Get
off the line. I've got to get the doctor. This is an
emergency.' Well, they knew him, and they knew this
was a lot of malarkey, so they would just keep right
on talking. He would be just jumping right up and
down, swearing and pounding things and clicking
phones, trying to disconnect them. Eventually he
would succeed and then he'd come on the line and
say, 'So-and-so women, nothing better to do than yap
away on the line all day.' He'd want the bank or
something like that. It wouldn't be an emergency.
And they'd all get back on the line as soon as he'd
hung up, and they all listened, of course, to what his
call was, and then they'd all give him a real hard time
and he'd stay on the line to hear this. Oh, it would get
really heated at times. The language would be dread-
ful, and I'd be listening, too. But, of course, you'd
miss some of it, some of the best of it, because you
would have to answer calls. You'd break away, answer
a few quick calls and come back on the line. They'd
all be talking at one another. It was wonderful."

Next in to see me was Pat. Like Gladdy, Pat used to be an operator. She was still working the board when the modern dial equipment came to town and made her obsolete. Coldwater got dial phones in 1962. The whole town assembled at the phone company office the night they switched over and watched the local member of parliament, MPP Lloyd A. Letherby, make the town's first dial long-distance call. He phoned his brother in California. Pat says she will never forget when the dial phones came to town.

"That was quite a big event in Coldwater, especially in the rural areas. It's hard to believe, but a lot of men were nervous about using a telephone back then. Then, when it went dial, they wouldn't touch it at all. You know, like it was something strange and different. I bet even today there are men in some rural areas that won't answer the telephone if their wife isn't around. They're just a little bit shy of it, I guess. They don't use it often enough. They felt more comfortable with it when there was an operator there. That's for sure. I think they liked to communicate with someone and talk to them rather than just operate a machine. It's still true, you know. I've heard several people say their husbands won't use the telephone ever since it went dial."

In 1962 when dial phones came to Coldwater, it cost $3.50 a month for a private line. The next major excitement in town was seventeen years later when the board of commissioners tried to raise the monthly rate by fifteen cents. They wanted to bump it from $3.50 to $3.65 a month. Linda Hass is the chairman of the Coldwater Municipal Phone Company. It is worth noting that Coldwater is the only phone company in Ontario and perhaps

all of Canada to have a woman chairman. Anyway, Linda
had just become active in the company when the rate
question bubbled to the surface. She was a commissioner
or something back then, elected, as she is today, by the
people in town. Linda sat opposite me in the lunch-room
and began to tell me about the meeting where the town,
for the second time in its history, rallied together and put
down its collective feet in the face of a hike in the monthly
phone bill.

"The meeting was electric. People didn't like the idea
of a rate increase at all. They were quite irate and
there was a lot of murmuring and rustling – altogether a very tense atmosphere. It was really very fright-
ening. I was wondering what I had done to get myself
into this mess. How could this happen to me? Just the
fact that we were sitting in the front and were sort of
the target for all those looks and feelings. It was a
super-charged atmosphere. The next day I felt like
everyone in town was looking at me. But I just held
my head up and talked to everyone as I usually do."

The rebels carried the day, and today in Coldwater it still
costs $3.50 a month for a private line in town. The rates
haven't gone up in twenty-three years. Not only is it
cheap, but if you are out of town when your bill comes
due, it's likely that Pat Orton in the front office will tell
Geraldine the treasurer and Roy the lineman that it's OK,
you are on vacation, and she's sure you'll drop in to pay as
soon as you get back.

It was getting late, and by now quite a crowd had
gathered in the small room to reminisce about their
phone company.

"It's almost supper," I said, looking at my watch.
"Perhaps we all should be going."

Before anyone left, however, I had two more questions.

I asked Linda, the chairman, how she thought the people in town felt about Coldwater Telephone.

"I think most people are proud of the system. They feel that we have something that is distinctly ours. We're not part of a huge conglomerate; this is our system. We may be a small village, and people come up from the city and say, oh, you know, 'these poor small-town people.' They sort of feel sorry for us, but they have no reason to because we have everything here. Everything. A lot more than any city person has. And to have our own phone system, it's special. We have something very distinctive and special for ourselves that's a success, a big success."

Everyone in the room was nodding. I turned to Ian, the manager, and asked my last question. I wanted to know what he thought would happen if Bell Canada came along and offered a whopping big sum of money to buy them all out. I wondered if the town would vote to sell to Bell.

"I sincerely hope not, and I cannot see it happening because the people in this town take a lot of pride in the fact that they own their own system. And in today's market that's quite an exception."

I shook hands with everyone, picked up my gear, and we all walked out together.

As everyone wandered towards their homes, I stood on the main street of Coldwater and looked at the railroad tracks and wondered how often a train came through town. I should phone home, I thought, as I stood by my car. I should call and let Linda know I'm running late. There was a phone booth on the other side of the street. I pulled a dollar out of my pocket and wandered into the hardware store and asked for four quarters. A minute later I was back again, this time asking for change for a quarter. It costs a dime to call home from Coldwater. Is there anywhere else in Canada where it only costs ten cents to make a phone call?

WHAT'S THE MATTER WITH RUBBER BOOTS?

I am wearing galoshes again. Big black dumpy rubber boots with a zippers that run up the front. And once again I am being maligned as a sartorial simpleton. Even people I barely know seem to delight in pointing out how ugly my boots are. Their aspersions drip with the implication that only an oaf would wear such . . . things. Members of my own family snorted in derision when I brought my galoshes home from the store. "You're not going to wear those tonight, are you?" asked my wife before a recent dinner party.

Well, yes. I am.

And I will wear them all winter long, thank you very much.

I have thrown out the boots I wore last winter. They were stretchy and extremely thin, sort of space-age things. They snapped over my shoes like surgical gloves. And they came with a pattern on top to disguise the fact that they were, in fact, boots. When I put them on they hugged my Hush Puppies and transformed them into a pair of sleek black Italian loafers. They kept me dry, but not warm.

Canadians have forsaken the overshoe – the rubber boot of our fathers. We have been sold down the river by retailers, fashion experts and our own insecurities. Goodbye buckles and zippers. Goodbye flaps and straps. Goodbye galoshes. Gone are the gaiters our grandfathers wore. Hello lined leather. Hello canvas sneaker. Hello thin leather soles. Hello stylish plastic, slippery as a banana peel. Hello leaky nylon. We walk out of shoe stores with new boots tucked stylishly under one arm and a fortune in waterproofing treatments under the other. We have become a nation of fashion plates who limp through winter with wet, frozen feet. We were once more sensible.

When I was a kid in Montreal West, little boys wore what they called strap-ons. They were brown and rubber and you put them over your shoes. They came halfway up your calves. There was a belt with a buckle that did up on the side. There was a cuff at the top made of real sheepskin. Guys like Sidney Bailey and Dougie Jones left their houses with their buckles open and the tops of their boots rolled down. They wore their rubber boots defiantly, like pirates. Guys like me had to make do by undoing the buckles slyly every morning, after we had rounded the corner off Brock onto Nelson Avenue, safely out of sight of home.

I never owned flight boots, though like most boys my age, I fought for them. Flight boots were the heavy, fleece-lined, double-zippered boots worn by British pilots in World War II. Perhaps it was out of respect for their origin that flight boots were worn belligerently, a size too large. You didn't as much walk as slop down the sidewalk. The soles never left the ground. The zippers were never closed.

"Time to start thinking about getting the rubbers out," Mom would say one October afternoon. Did she really do that? While I was at school, did she sit down with a coffee and *think* about getting the rubbers out?

They came out of a basement closet with a whiff of winter. People who love wine savour the moment when they pull out the cork. The inch of air that smokes out of the bottle is from France. It was sealed in there one autumn afternoon on a hillside in Burgundy. The older the air, the sweeter the pleasure.

Consider the secrets sealed in a rubber boot. Latex drips out of tropical trees like sap from a spring maple. Stepping into a rubber boot in February is like stealing a little part of Malaysia for your feet. Something to carry you through the snowdrifts. Something to keep your feet warm and dry. How could you possibly get wet in something that has been *vulcanized*? You could kill dragons in something that has been vulcanized.

When I was a boy, everyone in Montreal West owned rubber overshoes of some sort. There were even overshoes that would fit over women's high heels; they were made to accommodate up to three inches of heel. Women and children all wore boots that went over their ankles, but men had rubbers designed to keep only the soles of their shoes dry. Men wore boots that covered the soles and came up only one inch on either side of their shoes. They were boots that looked like dishes made for banana splits. Lawyers practised for hours in front of mirrors so they could step into these toe rubbers with elegant disregard. Most men had to hop around and reach out for walls as they struggled with their boots. At the Forum, in Montreal, it was these rubbers that came arcing out of the crowd, sailing over the ice at bum refs. The refs had to stoop in front of you and pick up your personal insult. It was a most satisfying protest.

These low-cut boots were a distinctly Canadian piece of gear. When the Miner Rubber Company of Granby, Quebec, was in full swing, they produced 800,000 pairs of them a year. The boots were known as Miner Crimp-Ons and were advertised coast to coast on television. When executives from B.F.Goodrich came from the States to visit their Quebec plant, they took cases of these Crimp-Ons home to give to their friends.

The Miner Rubber Company went out of business years ago; so did Woodstock Rubber. And Northern Rubber in Guelph. There are only two places left in Canada making rubber overshoes like the ones we used to wear – the Acton Rubber Company in Actonville, Quebec, and the Kaufman Family in Kitchener, Ontario. You wonder why there isn't as much snow as before? We aren't worthy of walking in it.

CAPITALISM BOILED DOWN

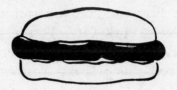

The Harvard Business School uses a teaching technique known as the case study method. Students at Harvard are presented with summaries of real business problems that real business executives have sweated over. Their assignment is to absorb the case study and propose solutions that might have worked in the real world. When they finish, they get to compare their ideas with what really happened.

You have just enrolled in the Stuart McLean School of Business. This is case one.

Ernie is a street vendor. He sells hotdogs from a wagon in downtown Toronto. He is probably the best hotdog salesman in the city. He may just be the best in the country. Like all good salesmen Ernie has a good feel for his product and he isn't shy to talk about it.

"The steamed hotdog was basically made famous in New York, and if you go down to New York City you'll find all of these hotdog vendors around Times

Square, outside the Penn Station. And people come from all over the world to have a steamed hotdog. Damon Runyon made them famous in a series of stories when some of the Runyon crew such as Rusty, Charlie and Harry the Horse used to run down to Times Square to get a steamed dog. Everybody started saying, we have to have a steamed dog. You know, what we tell people here is that this is a classic steamed dog. Buy one and you can almost picture yourself in New York City. You're almost there. You've got this steamed dog with sauerkraut and red sauce. And red sauce looks wonderful on white sauerkraut. It's like blood on snow, and the whole hotdog takes off. You bite into the dog and think of the vendors on Times Square, the theatre district and you know you can take people there. It's great stuff."

Ernie is so good at what he does that there are a substantial number of people in Toronto who are eating more hotdogs than they know they should. I know this because I am one of those people. Ernie sells his hotdogs where I teach, on the campus of the Ryerson Polytechnical Institute. He turned up one autumn with his stainless-steel hotdog wagon, and never left. He stayed, in fact, all winter. His tenacity made an impression on a number of people at Ryerson, including two of my students, Tim Richardson and Dean Askin.

"I remember thinking how weird it was seeing a guy selling hotdogs outside in the middle of the winter. It was so cold sometimes, and you don't see too many street vendors in the middle of the winter, especially standing out there all day. But Ernie did it, he was there, he was there for us."

"It's true, he was the only vendor in about a . . . well, in a forever block radius right throughout the cold weather. One day I saw him in the foyer taking five minutes to get warm, and then he went back out again, to sell more hotdogs. The man is remarkable. I don't know how he stood out there all winter in that cold, but he did, and people like him for it."

Ernie's stick-to-it-ness and delightful manner combined to win him a lot of customers. By the end of that first winter, his business, which had expanded steadily, was well established. By the time the weather warmed up that spring, he had a good thing going. Sure enough, it wasn't long after the snow melted that another vendor appeared and tried to move in on Ernie's territory.

Ernie is fifty-eight years old. We are going to call the competition the Young Guy. The Young Guy began setting up his cart every day right beside Ernie, and did his best to cut into Ernie's business.

The Young Guy lasted less than a week. Ernie blew him out of the water. You would go out at noon and see seven or eight people lined up in front of Ernie's wagon, and the Young Guy would be alone, clicking his hotdog tongs, trying in vain to attract business. One day he just didn't come back. Tip your hat to consumer loyalty and give round one to Ernie.

The second competitor showed up in the fall. But this time the competition was a little stiffer. A Greek restaurant owner named Chris set up his stall about a mustard squirt away from Ernie's wagon. Before long the gloves came off. Chris started a price war. He dropped the price of his dogs by twenty-five cents. Ernie consulted his financial backer, a man I know as Tony.

"We matched the price initially. OK, a quarter, all right, we can live with that. I think he went another

dime lower but we let him. It just didn't attract the
trade. I mean, all you have to do is taste the dogs.
Like I say, you get what you pay for. It didn't work
and he saw that it wasn't working so he brought his
prices back up to par."

Give round two to Ernie. In round one he blew away
the Young Guy. In round two, because of customer
loyalty, he was able to hold the line on prices.

You might have forgiven Ernie if he had started to
coast. He was firmly established, if you will excuse the
expression, as top dog on the campus and had successful-
ly turned away two assaults on his business. But it was at
this point that Ernie displayed the brilliance that makes
him one of the best hotdog salesmen in the country.
Instead of resting on his laurels, he began to do exactly
what the government says Canadian industry so often
neglects. Ernie started to invest in R and D. He set out to
improve his product.

"People think it's a simple product, but you have to
find the right wiener for the particular area you're
in. We've done that now, but we didn't start out with
the same wiener we have today. The other thing is,
you've got to match the bun. That took us almost five
months before we found a bun that went with the
wiener and was good for a steamed dog. Again, you
have to look at the way you're going to do it. If you
look at hotdogs, there are probably three major ways
they're done. One is boiling, two is steaming and
three is barbecuing. Boiling is a bad way of doing it
because you take the flavour out of the wiener.
Between the steaming and the barbecuing, steaming
keeps the flavour in. Barbecuing is OK but it tends to
dry out the wiener a little. But you've got to get a

wiener for the technique you're using, and then you've got to get a bun to match the wiener."

Ernie settled on the Chicago 58 wiener and an egg bun with poppy seeds. But he didn't stop there. He also expanded his line of condiments. By his second spring, along with mustard and ketchup, he was offering Dijon mustard, sauerkraut, grated Cheddar cheese and a tub of home-made barbecue sauce from a secret family recipe. He would mix up the barbecue sauce over the weekend and had usually run out of it by Wednesday. As a crowning touch, Ernie offered all his customers a candy from a candy dish, just like the fanciest of restaurants.

In the face of this onslaught, Chris the Greek hung tough, but he was left scrambling. He went to the Chicago 58 wiener, too, but didn't add the poppy seeds to his buns. When Ernie added the grated Cheddar, Chris added Kraft slices. As to the price, he went beyond acknowledging that Ernie set the lead. He went as far as denying that he had ever started a price war.

"I never dropped my price. There was no competition. No, we've got the same price, me and Ernie. Same price. We never fight, we're friends, that's all. I go with the price he puts; if he goes up, I go up, too. If he goes down, I go down. I got the cheese because he put the cheese. I have to. He got the barbecue sauce, he got the hot mustard, he got everything. But I don't think I'm gonna add the candy, no."

Then one morning Chris the Greek upped the ante. He showed up with a gas barbecue on his wagon. Everyone was stunned. Including Ernie. Face it. A barbecue is classy. It not only smells good, it also has a certain rustic romance. Above all, it is good for business. For the first time ever, Chris started to attract customers.

Remember, this is a case study, right? Well, we have come
to the test part. If you are Ernie, what do you do about
the barbecue? Are your goodwill, your grated Cheddar,
your poppy seed buns and your candy dish enough to pull
you through this? Or do you go out and buy a barbecue
for your wagon? If you stick with your steamer, are you
going to see all your customers go up in smoke?

Do you dance with the girl what brung you?

Or do you buy a brand-new gas barbecue?

Before you read Ernie's strategy, you should pause
here and decide on your answer. Here is Ernie's:

"Remember, if you are in a leadership position and
the other people are following you, the day you
follow them, that means they're in the leadership
position. So for me to put a barbecue on my wagon
means I would be following Chris. We won't do that.
When we do something it has to be one step above
him. We consider ourselves leaders."

Ernie held the line. He didn't buy the barbecue.

About a month after he made that decision, I went, at
lunch, and sat on the grass and watched the two wagons
for about half an hour. I went as an empirical scientist. I
counted customers. In thirty minutes Ernie had thirty-
three clients. Chris had twelve. As well as statistical
information, just like any self-respecting sociologist, I
collected anecdotal material. Lorri Neil and Laurie Gillies
are students at Ryerson.

"It was about two weeks ago and it was a really nice
day and some friends and I went to get a hotdog.
There were about four people lined up at Ernie's
wagon, but nobody was at the other guy's. So there
were three of us and we looked over at the other guy
and thought, well, too bad. We're gonna have Ernie

dogs. So now there's seven people lined up at
Ernie's, right? So we waited. It didn't matter. The
other guy must have felt bad but it just didn't matter
because we were willing to wait for Ernie
dogs – steamed or not, who cares about a barbecue? I
don't want a charcoal dog, anyway."

"I wouldn't go to the other guy at all. I mean,
Ernie was there all the time. All winter. I'd feel
disloyal if I went to the other guy. And it may sound
silly over a stupid hotdog, but I'd go to Ernie over
anybody else."

Ernie's continuing strong market position can be
explained in a variety of ways. First, barbecue or no
barbecue, there is much about Ernie's wagon to recom-
mend it. He has the grated *Cheddar* cheese, the *poppy* seed
buns, the *home-made* chili sauce and the *complimentary*
candy. All things considered, it could be argued that he
has a superior product. But it goes beyond that. The
question of reliability has to be considered. Ernie showed
up all winter. No one else was prepared to stand on the
sidewalk in January, and people feel that sort of persever-
ance deserves to be rewarded. Finally there is the matter
of service. Chris does a workmanlike job of selling
hotdogs. He serves them up with competence. Ernie,
however, has style. He has created a world. A world of
steam and secret barbecue sauce, peopled by a fraternity
of regulars who come back every day to buy their lunch
from the world's greatest hotdog salesman. It's a world
Ernie says he loves.

"What can I tell you. There's a lot of nice people in
my world. We all meet around the central theme of
what's new with hotdogs [Ernie laughs]. And so we
always have to think of another story about a hotdog,

and we come around one way or another. It's fun
because there's no structure to it. We get all sorts of
people around here and we can always kid them a bit.
Some things they believe and some they don't. We're
the magic deli of hotdogs, that's what we are."

No one really knows who Ernie is. He is a bit of a mystery.
Tony, his boss, says he showed up one day wearing a suit
and carrying a briefcase and asked him for a job. At first
Tony thought he was a city inspector and was a little leery
of hiring him. Now he wishes he had ten other guys like
him. He looks like an ex-fighter or a stevedore, or
someone who spent time with the French Foreign Legion.
I know that Ernie is not his real name. It's a nickname one
of the students gave him. He tells me that he used to sell
semiconductor computer parts for some multinational
corporation. He probably did. Ernie could sell anything.

SMITTEN BY SALMON

This is my all-time favourite fish story. It falls, I suppose, under the category of "The One That Got Away", and though that may be a well-worn theme, there is nothing familiar about the fish and fishermen in this saga. It is the story of what happened when three giant American corporations decided to go salmon fishing. It begins in the late seventies when American fish consumption was, as they say in the boardrooms, "trending up". Well, actually, it begins before that. Its origins lie in the simple idea of the trout farm.

Almost everyone has heard about trout farming. Instead of the uncertain old-fashioned way of catching trout with a hook and worm, trout farmers raise trout in water-filled pens where they are fed like cattle on a feedlot.

Trout farms worked so well that somewhere, someone had the bright idea to do the same thing with salmon. Except they went one better. Why not, they reasoned, raise salmon like Texas steers. Look after them in a hatchery while they are babies, but as soon as they are old enough, send them into the open ocean to "graze" where the food is cheap. After a few years, the reasoning went, the salmons' innate homing instinct would bring them home, fat and fully grown. Then all that would be left to do would be to pluck them out of the water and pop them into cans. An elegant and profitable venture. No fuss, no muss. Which is why the directors of the Campbell Soup Company, British Petroleum and Weyerhaeuser all thought they had found a sure thing. Here's what one industry advocate said:

> "On a piece of paper, when you look at numbers, costs and investments and the like, it becomes a viable concept with as little as 2 percent return. And remember, you're dealing with a very high-quality product here because you aren't capturing them with a hook or a net. They're just going to come back to you like a puppy dog, if you will. So there would be no bruise marks. They would just be high-quality fish. I think everybody looked at it and said; 'God, this is something we ought to try,' and we did. And everyone, I think, assumed success."

It seemed foolproof. The figures were so seductive, the idea was unassailable. If you released 100,000 smolts (baby salmon), you only needed 200 of them to come home, and you would be makin' bacon. You can almost hear them smacking their lips in the boardrooms.

Here's what happened.

Campbell Soup was first into the water. Overcome with enthusiasm, they started chucking millions of smolts into a west coast river that flows into the Pacific Ocean. According to the textbooks, a few short years later, plump salmon would swim back up that river to spawn. As Campbell Soup executives sat around, totting up profits, no doubt, word arrived from the coast that the baby salmon – the millions of baby salmon – had made it to the ocean where they had been greeted by a convention of hungry west coast seals. Randolph Earle was in charge of the salmon program for Campbell Soup.

"I'm not sure we as humans give animals as much credit for their mental capabilities as they deserve. It's kind of interesting that once a seal finds out there's a free lunch somewhere, or there's a whole lot of fish that are accessible, sooner or later there will be more than one seal hanging around."

Down the coast a way, British Petroleum (yes, the oil company) also leapt into the water with both feet. And they, too, experienced seal problems. Before long BP statisticians figured out that seals were getting upward of 60 percent of their smolts only hours after they were released. But BP wasn't prepared to roll over and die. They assembled a task force of the best minds in corporate America and charged them with the job of outsmarting the seals. The task force came up with a sure-fire solution. They designed two high-frequency sound boxes that could be submerged in the estuary where their baby salmon hit the ocean. The boxes were designed to emit a high-pitched noise that seals would find so horrible, they wouldn't come near the bay. BP's experts glibly predicted that the bay would be virtually seal-free. The baby salmon, they smugly said, would have a fighting chance.

The sound boxes were put in place, the switches flipped on, the next batch of baby salmon released and . . . instead of the seal-free bay they expected, the BP experts stood sheepishly along the shore of a bay full of seals swimming around with their heads out of the water. The seals obviously found the noise unpleasant, but they were managing to dunk their heads underwater every time a mouthful of baby salmon swam by.

Give rounds one and two to the seals.

Give round three to the common murre.

The common murre is a sea-bird. There are about half a million adult murres off the west coast of the United States – at least that's what BP's chief salmon rancher, Ernie Lewis, figures.

"Each of these adult birds requires a daily ration of a half-pound of fish. Which is a tremendous biomass of fish that this population consumes on a daily basis just to maintain itself. Some of the field studies that we have done suggest that we're losing as many as 50,000 or 60,000 smolts daily from Yaquina Bay alone. And if you multiply this out over a season, that represents a very high percentage of the total amount of smolts that we are releasing, just due to that one predator alone."

One year someone thought it would be a good idea to release the baby salmon in September, after the sea-birds had migrated for the winter. They figured that if they held the smolts until after the birds had gone, they would at least avoid one predator. Everyone agreed that this seemed to make a lot of sense. However, when they finally let the fish go, and we are talking about five million baby fish here, something went terribly wrong. The fish seemed to get confused. So confused, in fact, that instead of turning left and swimming towards the ocean, they turned right and headed for the hills. That spring in the Oregon mountains when the black bears woke up and stumbled down to the creek, they couldn't believe their eyes. They thought they had died and gone to bear heaven.

Anyone involved with these early efforts would, I think, agree that things didn't work out quite as smoothly as expected. In fact, a dispassionate observer could fairly conclude that all that really happened was that corporate America had spent a lot of time and money spoon-feeding west coast seals, birds and bears. But these guys were committed to their idea and were convinced that if they could just get it right, everyone would be rich. Which led to the next problem. They ran out of salmon eggs.

Lesser men might have thrown in the towel at this point. Our heroes soldiered on. They bought ten million salmon eggs from the Soviet Union. Then they coddled those eggs into smolts in their hatcheries and, on an auspicious spring afternoon, released eight million communist baby salmon into American waters. The smolts did what you might expect communist salmon to do. They defected. The returns were, as Randolph Earle put it, disappointing.

"I think the disappointment was fairly high, but on the other hand, since it was not a well-understood technology at that time, there was still the hope that OK, they didn't come back this year, maybe they'll come back next year. I think where the biggest disappointment came in was when they didn't come the next year, or even the year after that."

Of the 8 million Soviet salmon that were released to graze off the coast of America, 7 undersized males returned. I should be clear here. That is not 7 million or 700,000 or even 700. That's 7 as in 1, 2, 3, 4, 5, 6, – 7! At this point Campbell and Weyerhaeuser folded up their tents and left town. BP said they still weren't ready to call it a day. Randolph Earle, who worked for Campbell, said he understood why BP would want to keep plugging.

"The key impression that we probably want to leave with people is not that this is a dumb idea, because we are not convinced that it is a dumb idea. Apparently we were doing something wrong. We just hadn't thought of it, learned it, or whatever. We were missing part of the concept and hadn't made it work. But it does seem viable that you could make it go. I hope I'm not sounding just like a dreamer. Do you know what I mean?"

BP had another idea up their sleeves. A twist that they believed could finally turn things around. It's an idea that people came to refer to as the Dunkirk of salmon ranching. BP built a submersible barge that could float under the surface of the ocean. They have begun to use this underwater cage to ferry baby salmon out of the estuary and through the lines of hungry seals and ravenous shore birds.

"Basically the fish are placed in this barge, which is almost a square box, you might say. And we can haul upward of 100,000 smolts per trip. It's towed through the water at about 5 miles per hour. Basically the fish are towed out and when we get at some distance, usually between 4 and 20 miles, we release the fish. We simply release the tailgate which flops down. The fish then evacuate the barge and scatter."

BP is still not sure if their barge is the answer to their problems. They say they are quietly optimistic. Of course, they have said that before. And you know what is driving them crazy? The Japanese and the Soviet Union have been salmon ranching for years. They get a 7 to 8 percent return. Go figure that.

NORMAN VINCENT PEALE, MEET JOE GIRARD

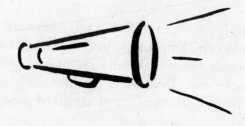

The night was advertised as an opportunity to listen to two of the world's most sought-after speakers. Two men who, said the ads, "motivate, inspire and inform". A double bill to end all double bills. The opening act would be Dr Norman Vincent Peale. The most influential clergyman in the United States of America. The man who coined the phrase *and* wrote the book – Mr *Power of Positive Thinking*. And Dr Peale was just the warm-up act. After the intermission we would meet, and it says so in the *Guinness Book of Records*, the World's Greatest Salesman, a used-car dealer from Detroit called Joe Girard. How could I pass up a night like that?

I settled into my seat at Roy Thomson Hall and waited with the capacity crowd for the lights to dim. Suddenly, almost magically, the room grew still and Dr Peale stepped, positively, from the wings and literally bounced across the stage to warm and sustained applause. I checked my watch. He was five minutes late.

I had never laid eyes on Norman Vincent Peale before. The program said he was born in 1898 and if that is true he looked remarkably fit for his age. From the balcony he seemed a benign owl of a man. If Elmer Fudd came to life, went to a speech therapist, was cured and, as a testament to that miracle was born again, you would have Norman Vincent Peale. He spoke without a note for fifty minutes. The audience was mesmerized.

"Shoot for the moon," he said, "because if you miss the moon you will land among the stars. Get down on your knees every night and say, 'Lord, thank you for my problems.' Because a problem is not a burden and a positive thinker is not afraid of problems. Pain, hardship and sorrow are the resistance of life, and resistance makes the muscles strong. A problem is like exercise for the spirit. The only people who don't have problems are dead people. You are going to have problems until the day you die, and if you have ten problems you are twice as alive as the poor miserable apathetic slob who only has five problems. And if you should wake up one morning and say, 'I don't have any problems,' then look out. Cause you've got a problem. You may be on your way out. Problems is what grows them big."

Norman Vincent Peale is into imagery. Anything you can "image" is within your grasp. You can become what you imagine yourself to be. That is the *power* of positive thinking. You have to stand in front of your mirror and look long and hard into the glass and say, "I *am* some-body." A sideways glance won't do. And if you don't be-lieve you *are* somebody, then say, "I am going to *be* somebody" – and believe that!

Norman Vincent Peale is the original. The mould from whence cometh Robert H. Schuller and all the other Hour of Power TV evangelists who preach success through faith. Jesus, they say, wants us all to be prosperous. It is a seductive and appealing notion, and Norman Vincent Peale is an attractive and righteous salesman. It is, however, worth remembering that he is also the man who toured the United States in 1960 warning that the cultural fabric of the nation was at stake if a Roman Catholic like John Kennedy were to be elected to the White House.

Not many people at Roy Thomson Hall were giving much thought to Dr Peale's politics. They embraced him with the enthusiasm such crowds usually reserve for an overtime goal. I was a little surprised by the open exuberance. I thought that going to hear Norman Vincent Peale would be a little like going to the self-help section of a book store. It is something that you just don't want to be caught doing. You don't want your kids to catch you thumbing through something called *Effective Parenting*. If they know you are reading stuff like that, they are going to start rolling their eyes every time you say something earnest. I thought perhaps you'd go to another city if you wanted to hear Norman Vincent Peale. Sort of like having an affair. I thought, I guess, that people might be embarrassed to be there.

I was wrong.

People felt GOOD about being there.

They felt POSITIVE about being there.

This was a salon full of salesmen. Or so I learned when I approached some of the audience during intermission.

"I was the top Remax salesman in North America a couple of years ago. Norman Vincent Peale is someone whose books I have been reading for an awfully long time, and it's just a thrill to think that I can hear someone like him speak in person.''

There were salesmen from just about every city within a day's drive. I met a TV salesman from Sudbury, a car salesman from Hamilton, a real estate broker from Mississauga and, my personal favourite, an undertaker from Toronto.

"I sell death. Or maybe I should say I deal in death and sell myself, and that's why I am here tonight. I want to get motivated to sell myself better because a funeral parlour is a business, you know. We are in the Yellow Pages and we have competitors. Every person in business, whether it's in my business or not, has days when they get a bit down, and if they start thinking along the lines that Dr Peale has told us about, well, that becomes helpful. It's our job to raise the spirits of people that are down, and I think a funeral director can learn something from anybody. I sincerely believe that. Especially a used-car salesman of the calibre of Joe Girard.''

The lobby lights flashed. Intermission was over. We all settled back in our seats and were whispering to one another when Joe Girard suddenly roared onto the empty stage like a crazed banshee. He came on so full of attitude that he made Norman Vincent Peale look unsure of himself.

There was a single lectern on the stage at Roy Thomson Hall which, if you have ever been there, is a polite theatre. It's the sort of place to which you might want to wear a tie or a dress. A hall more accustomed to ballet than ballyhoo. Before long, Joe Girard was crawling over the lectern like it was a fire hydrant and he was an unpleasant little dog. At one point he actually stood on the lectern and howled at the people in the front row.

Joe never graduated from high school, and he sounds like it. If the Fonz went on the self-help circuit, people would say he was copying Joe Girard. He is not your run-of-the-mill after-dinner speaker. But he is, undoubtedly (as he would be happy to tell you), the Best Salesman in the World. And he did tell us. Several times.

In 1973 Joe sold 1,425 cars. That's an average of 6 cars every working day. That same year, according to Joe, the average car salesman in the United Sates moved 7 cars a *month*; 1973 was the year you had to make an appointment to buy a car from Joe Girard.

He swaggered around the stage and told us that if you want to move a lot of cars you have to have P.M.A. That's Positive Mental Attitude. Joe says he has so much P.M.A. that sometimes he is afraid that is is going to explode. There were moments during his presentation when I thought we were about to see that happen.

P.M.A., said Joe, means if your customer says "no", he means "maybe". If he says "maybe", he means "yes".

"You have to oil your confidence machine," he cooed. "You only got to want. Want is the power. It is the gas that drives you and your machine to the top. The whole secret of life is to know what you want. Let me tell ya what I do first thing in the morning. I run to my mirror and I look into it real close and I say, 'Somebody is gonna pay for getting this kid out of bed today.'"

After the show I ran up to Joe with my tape recorder and asked him to tell me one more time what he does in the morning.

"Before I leave the house I look into the mirror. It's a full-length mirror, and I look at my body, and I look at the little sign I have on the mirror and the sign says, 'Would I buy you today?' And I look in my attitude machine, my confidence machine, I look at my clothes, I look at everything about me, and unless I can look in the mirror and say, 'Yes, I am ready, Joe, to go out for this day that God gave me,' – if I can't say that – I go back to bed. But if I can, if I am really ready, then I open the door, and I scream inside of my body, 'I feel good, I feel great, I am number one.' And then I open up the door and holler out within my body and say, 'Look out, world, I'm coming out one more time.' "

It seems the mirror gets a lot of work in the positive thinking business.

As Joe built to his climax I was struck by the image of funeral directors all over southern Ontario spending their evenings in front of their bathroom mirrors visualizing *my* death so they could get my business. The notion of undertakers bursting out onto their driveways in the morning full of the kind of enthusiasm that Joe was pitching filled me with apprehension. I could see them wrestling people into coffins. If I can imagine it happening, does that mean it will?

Suddenly I was aware that Joe was asking people to come down onto the stage. He wanted three people to come down. He had gold pins that said NUMBER ONE that he would give to people who would come down and stand on the stage and scream, at the top of their lungs:

"I FEEL GOOD!"

"I FEEL GREAT!"

"I AM NUMBER ONE!"

"If you put the gold pin in your lapel," said Joe, "You'll see it shining in the light out of the corner of your eye."

Twenty people came down onto the stage. Joe lined

them up in a row so they were facing the audience like a chorus line. Then he passed the microphone down the row and one by one each person took a step forward and said:

"I feel Good!"

"I feel Great!"

"I am Number One!"

No one yelled with quite the gusto that Joe wanted until the microphone was passed to a sensible-looking gentleman in a blue suit. He could have been a little league coach somewhere. Or maybe your neighbour. When it was his turn with the microphone, he was so excited he ripped off his suit jacket and, screaming, "I AM NUMBER ONE" at the top of his lungs, whirled the jacket around and around over his head like a stripper and flung it into the audience. There was a moment of stunned silence as the jacket arched out over the crowd like a giant bird. It must have landed about twenty-five rows from the stage. By the time it came down, everyone was on their feet cheering and clapping just like they had for Joe, and the little league coach was standing on the stage grinning and shaking Joe Girard's hand like a mad fool.

I sometimes wonder if he ever got the coat back.

NO PLACE CALLED HOME

I met Anne at the Scott Mission at ten o'clock on a Thursday morning. Anne goes to the mission every morning at ten for lunch. There were four hundred other people in the room when I met her, sharing soup, potatoes and peas at long institutional tables. Four hundred people down on their luck. The gentleman who was showing me around made a point of mentioning that most of the people in the lunch-room didn't have trouble with alcohol, but it was clear that he wasn't talking about Anne.

I recognized Anne as one of the shaky women and unshaven men I have seen for years, hovering around liquor stores across this country, usually dirty and always trying to scratch together enough spare change for another bottle of cheap booze. I wanted to talk to her because one evening, brushing by a group of what we have come to call winos, I suddenly realized that I did not think of them as individuals. I couldn't imagine them as ever having been children, or as fathers or mothers or anything other than the drunk who stumbled up to me asking for spare change.

I wanted to know how one person had ended up like this.

Like everyone else, when I am asked for money by people like Anne, sometimes I give and sometimes I don't. I have no idea what makes me generous one day and uptight another. Somehow, I thought talking to Anne would help me figure that out. Or at least help me figure out whether I should or shouldn't be giving anything at all.

It was only ten in the morning, but Anne had already been drinking for seven hours. She had begun drinking when she had left her girlfriend's house at three that morning. She had fallen asleep on the couch the previous night, and when she woke up at three, she went out looking for her boyfriend. She found him, as she thought she would, sleeping in the doorway of a bank. She woke him, and they started to drink.

I asked her if I could turn on my tape recorder, and when she said yes, I asked her how much she had drunk so far that day.

"I started off with a couple of beers, and then I went over to Queen Street. They have a store there where you can buy bitters [an alcoholic infusion of herbs, used as a stimulant for the stomach, which is sold in many grocery stores]. OK, so I drank that, and then at six-thirty I drank two beers and maybe five or six more bottles of bitters. That's just to calm myself down from the previous day's drunk. You know, that levels me off."

It is cold in Toronto in January, and Anne was wearing a brown wool toque and a ripped sheepskin jacket over a windbreaker and sweater. She remained fully dressed the entire time we sat talking in the mission. Everything about her was dirty. Her hands looked like she had been gardening or working on a machine. There were round sores on her wrists. She said she had been taking penicillin for the sores but it wasn't working on account of all the alcohol in her blood. Her hair was stringy. Her face was streaked. Her jacket was stained. She told me she had no home and lived on the street. If she hadn't fallen asleep at her girlfriend's, she could just as easily have spent the night on the ground or, like her boyfriend, in the doorway of some bank. She told me all this in a matter-of-fact way. She is in her early thirties and has a young, almost innocent face. She has not, however, been living an innocent life.

> "The people in the circle I am with, like when the liquor stores and everything else are over, they'll drink Lysol. You mix it with water – five parts water, one part Lysol. And, like, the drink really tastes lousy, but it keeps the drunk going. Cause it hurts when the drunk starts coming off. It hurts a lot."

Anne grew up in a middle-class neighbourhood and did well in school. She graduated from grade thirteen, married and had two children – a girl who is now twelve and a boy who is three. To begin with, she and her husband sold jewellery on the street. Her husband told me that of the two of them, it was Anne who was more ambitious. It was Anne who started making and selling her own jewellery in place of the stuff they bought wholesale, and it was Anne who got the two of them off the street and into the store. Anne told me they owned half of the store and were doing rather well, rather early in their lives.

> "We had an exclusive jewellery boutique by the time I was twenty-five. I designed my own jewellery ... geez, that was about six years ago. But it was a good

business. The mall it was in appeals to the more upper-class type of person. The business is still operating; it's in the hands of my ex-business partner. He's very well-to-do. He has a house on Bayview, in a yuppie sort of area."

Everything had to be perfect when Anne was working in the store. She wore designer clothes and would fuss over her nails. She wore a size five dress and there were dresses that she bought and never wore, because when she got· them home and tried them on, they somehow were just not right. I don't know how happy her marriage was, but while she was still living at home she had an affair with another man. The affair lasted for some years and at some point her husband found out and at another point she started drinking. She said her husband threw her out when he found out about the affair. He said he asked her to leave when her drinking became so hideous that social services threatened to take the kids. This was the only moment where they remembered things differently. It doesn't really matter. The important thing is that once upon a time there was an attractive young woman who lived with her kids and her husband in an apartment with a colour TV and a VCR and a washing machine and a dishwasher; and that young woman used to get dressed up and do her nails and go to work selling jewellery in a jewellery store in a mall in downtown Toronto. She made between $600 and $800 a week. And then something happened.

"I really started getting drunk. But people were used to me being an upper-class lady, so people pretended not to notice. I just made sure I'd be chewing gum or something like that, so they couldn't smell it on my breath. I thought I was fooling everybody, but everybody knew. When you're in that condition you don't realize that other people know. You don't realize at all, and you keep drinking because the feeling, it keeps you from hurting, you know, as much.''

You already know that this story does not have a happy ending. Anne and her husband sold their half of the jewellery business to their partner. Anne got $4,000 in cash. So did her husband. When she left home she could drink forty ounces of rum a day, and her $4,000 didn't last long. She lived first with one man, a friend. Then with another. And then in a series of cheaper and cheaper apartments and rooms. It took three years for her life to unravel completely.

Now she lives on the street panhandling for spare change. She says there have been a few times, when she has been too sick to beg, that she has called her husband and he has given her twenty dollars for booze. She says he understands. He says he has tried to get her help but she always walks away from it. She says that she is worried that her family doesn't have the money they used to have when she was working, and that she has tried to get the business going again. She said that last summer she tried to sell jewellery on the street again, but she just couldn't seem to handle it.

"I felt very, very guilty because the family was used to $600 to $800 a week income, plus extras. And they were being cut down to maybe $250 a week. But I was living in a little rooming house at the time and it had cockroaches, and it was cold, and it was noisy. Oh, it was awful. You had to share a bathroom, which was really dirty, but you know something? You get used to it. Like at first it was such a shock. I thought I was going to die. But now I'm used to it. I don't even have to live anywhere now.''

These days if Anne needs to go somewhere, she will get on a bus and tell the driver that she has no money. She says mostly they let her travel for free and, looking at her, I guess I would, too, if I was a bus driver. I asked her where she got the coat she was wearing. She told me a girlfriend had given it to her about a week ago.

"It's really a shabby one," she said. "Like, I was going to get a new one today. When you sleep in your clothes, right, you've got to get a lot of different ones. It didn't fit or anything, but I'm just not as particular as I used to be."

"It's an old sheepskin coat," I said.

"Yes."

"It was a nice coat one day."

"Geez," she replied, almost surprised, "it was even nice last week. I've been sleeping on the ground, and my boyfriend beat up a few people yesterday so I got a lot of blood on it."

"That's how you got the blood on the sleeve?" I asked.

"Oh, yeah, I had to pull him off people." There was a pause and we looked at each other without saying anything. I tried to ask the next question kindly.

"So, what's your future, Anne?"

"I think I'm probably going to die in a year or two, or else I'm going to straighten out, but I don't see myself straightening out. It really doesn't matter. As long as my children are set up, I've done my responsibilities to the world. So if I ruin my own life it's my life to ruin, that's all."

"You sound like you might be looking forward to that," I said slowly.

"I've become a bit suicidal. I guess this is a slow way of going, rather than, you know, cutting your

throat or something. And I have some good times.
Yesterday was a rough day because my boyfriend was
very violent. He got into a violent drunk. But when
you get into a happy drunk we probably have more
fun than you would. Maybe today will be a day like
that." Again we looked at each other quietly. Then in
the silence I heard myself asking the question that
had brought me there.

"Can I do anything to help you out?" I asked.
There was a pause, and though Anne was laughing
when she answered, there was no missing the pain in
her laughter.

"Five dollars?" she asked, her voice trailing off.
"That's all I go for. Can you give me five dollars?"

I didn't know what to do. We looked at each other for
nearly a minute. Our eyes locked together, not blinking.
She looked away first. I gave her the five dollars and put
my tape recorder away. Then I walked along Dundas
Street with Anne and her five friends. I was with them for
an hour. In that hour they drank a bottle of rubbing
alcohol and sniffed glue from a metal tin. It was snowing
and too cold for me in the bus shelter where they were
standing, so I left them.

No one has asked me for spare change since.

THE REAL SQUEEZE

I was peeling along the 401 on my way to London, Ontario, to break the law. I had a rendezvous in a restaurant with four people I had never met and whose names I didn't know. They were fanatic cavers who, said a friend, satisfied their urge for dark, damp places by sometimes spelunking in the city's storm sewers. In a foolish moment I had agreed to go "sewer caving" with them. I had forgotten to mention my fear of dark, damp places.

By the time I had left the highway and found the restaurant, I was feeling the kind of uneasiness that lurks just this side of panic. I walked inside wondering why I kept putting myself in situations I knew I wasn't going to enjoy.

I had been told I would have no trouble recognizing my hosts. And I didn't. They were the only people in the restaurant with miners' hats and oil lamps on their table. It would be better, they explained, if we waited in the restaurant until it got dark. I nodded, smiled nervously and sat down at their table.

Now. I want you to imagine something.

Imagine you are the first person to get into a small elevator. As you stand against the back wall, the elevator fills so completely that you are pushed uncomfortably into the people around you. Just as the doors are about to close, two more people squeeze aboard. You are now pinned against the back wall vaguely wondering about things like maximum loads. Your arms are trapped by your sides. The elevator begins to move. Suddenly it shudders, sighs and stops dead. There is a momentary pause. Then the lights go out. It is crowded, getting hot, and it is pitch-black. You can't raise your arms to your face, and even if you could, you wouldn't see them. How are you feeling?

This is the sort of situation that my hosts thrive on. On summer weekends they drive as far as Tennessee and back to explore caves. But simply being underground isn't enough for them. Caving, they tell me, isn't really fun unless you are afraid. A fun time for this group is to go into the bowels of the earth and find a tunnel too tiny to fit through, and then *try to fit through it*. They call this "doing a squeeze".

I asked Paul, who was sipping a beer and grinning at me from across the table, to describe a typical squeeze.

"It's a hole perhaps a foot high and maybe six to eight feet wide – just big enough to worm your body through. You're not on your knees, you're on your belly, worming like a bug. And there's no room even to have a hard hat on. You've taken your hard hat off and you're pushing it ahead of you. At first it's OK, but as you get closer to the end, it's so narrow that it's gripping your chest. You're lying flat on your chest and the ceiling is so low that it's touching your back. Then you try to take a deep breath so you can push harder, and you can't. You feel the weight of millions of tons of rock on your chest and on your back, and it feels as though it's *squeezing* you. Your lamp is burning low and people behind you are expecting you to go on and they are sweating and they start to push. If you start to panic, you're done. All your friends are going to spend the next forty-five minutes calming you down so you'll relax and unlodge your chest, because if you just exhale, you'll be free.''

Paul explained that you usually find squeezes two or three miles into a cave. By then, he reassured me, it is not only completely dark, but you are also basically lost. Apparently once you are two or three miles into a cave, you never really know your way out.

I volunteered that the notion of being lost in a cave and then setting off down a branch line the size of a rabbit hole so that I could be both lost and stuck, was not the most pleasant way I could imagine spending my free time. Paul and his friends smiled at me the way devotees of a religious cult might smile at a new recruit they have picked up at a bus station cafeteria. Then someone wondered, too casually, I thought, if I would like to see *their* cave. This caught me off guard. I had, against my better instincts, already agreed to join them on a sewer trek. I was wearing my boots and old clothes, because they had warned me about the water and the dirt. No one had said anything about a cave.

I soon learned that my new friends are so mesmerized by caves, that they have talked the curator of a local museum into letting them build him a nine-hundred square-foot concrete cavern. Their simulated cave has been such a box office success that the director has let them keep a key to the museum so they can visit their exhibit after hours. What they didn't tell me, as we headed for the museum, is that they have built a private tunnel they like to play in. It is more a burrow, really – a chute with the circumference of a flower pot. It's their own private squeeze, and they wanted me to crawl through it.

We were looking at the opening by the flickering light of our gas miners' hats, and I was telling Paul that I didn't think I could fit through his hole even if he greased me. Paul was smiling again. He explained that I was looking at the wide part of the squeeze. It takes a turn to the right, he said reassuringly, and then dwindles to about half the size. He smiled again, dropped to his knees and disappeared into the hole like a seal slipping through the ice. I stumbled ten yards down the corridor and stuck my head into the other end of the rat hole, where I could see him inching towards me. He was grunting and groaning as if he was being beaten.

I have this vague memory from years ago of my father trying to drag me, against my will, into Dr MacDermot's office. I have my heels planted in Dr MacDermot's front lawn. I am screaming at the top of my lungs. I know that if I let my father get me through the door, Dr MacDermot is going to give me what used to be referred to as a booster shot. I did not, as a kid, like needles.

That was then. This is now. Now I don't like small dark places. I did not want to go down the hole. I didn't want to die wedged in a concrete tube, even if it was in a museum. But there were four of them and one of me. I was outnumbered and beginning to sense that I was doomed.

"Stuck is only a frame of mind," said Paul with his hand pushing firmly down on my shoulder. "You won't get stuck if you don't think you will. You'll figure out how to dislocate your shoulders and things like that, tricks to shorten your body and make it narrower. Anyway, on with it. Away you go now."

It took me about forty-five minutes to worm my way through the thirty-foot tunnel. Halfway along, I froze and found myself lying in the darkened museum thinking about a fraternity initiation I'd once read about where things had gone horribly wrong. The fraternity brothers told the bound and blindfolded inductee, who they had laid out on a table, that they were going to cut out his heart. Then they pressed an icicle onto his chest and he had a heart attack. As I wedged my body through the squeeze, I could feel the icicle pressing on my chest. When I finally summoned up the courage to make the final assault on the narrow exit, I got stuck at the shoulders, but eventually popped out like an old pro. Fear, and then the release from fear, said Paul, is one of the attractions of caving.

> "It's the fear in the pit of your stomach. You're so gripped that your senses become hyper-acute, and that's what I long for. I push my limits every time I go caving. Each time I go into a cave I hope to reach new plateaus of fear. Frankly I'm not very worried that I'm going to die. I go to be consumed by that strange awareness that comes with fear. Failure is part of it, too. Sometimes you reach a point where you're so overcome with your own emotion that you back down. But that's part of the experience. Then you go back to whatever it was that defeated you to see if you can do it the next time."

We left the museum and drove quietly across town to the banks of the Thames River. We parked our cars in an industrial parking lot and crossed a field in the dark to a place where a large storm sewer empties into the river. After the squeeze, the sewer seemed luxurious. It was a concrete tube about four feet in diameter. Large enough to walk right into, but small enough so that we had to walk hunched over. There was about three inches of water running along the bottom of the tunnel as we splashed into the darkness. The water, pushing against our feet, made it feel as if we were walking up a stream. Our miners' lamps flickered on the sewer walls. We had to climb over a few quasi-waterfalls as we moved up from one level of sewer to the next. My guides told me that sometimes they come across animals on these hikes, once a nesting bird, once a family of raccoons. We walked for about half an hour, mostly in silence, until the concrete pipe abruptly ended, and we stepped into a spacious section of sewer where we could stand. Instead of the concrete tube, the walls here were made of brick. The ceiling was vaulted. It had the feel of a wine cellar on the Côtes du Rhône. No one said anything for about five minutes. Then Ted kicked at the water.

"This is the most interesting section of sewer I've ever been in. The rest of them are cement tubes, but this one reminds me of the black-and-white movie where the Phantom of the Opera ran through the sewers of Paris. I think it's the romance that attracts me to this part. It's about eight feet high and maybe twelve feet wide. There's rough concrete on the floor with three inches of water running down to the river, but from about two feet up it is all arched brick. It looks like a miniature railway tunnel, but it reminds me of the Tennessee caves. That's why I like it here. It's like being in a cave."

Recently, in Toronto, two children who were hiking through the sewer system died when they were overcome by some sort of sewer gas. My guides told me that, yes, that was possible. Methane gas can leak from the sewage system into the storm sewers. And that's not the only danger. Chemicals, either gas or liquid, are often

dumped into the sewers, sometimes accidently, sometimes on purpose. There is also, said Paul, the danger
of a sudden storm raising the water level in the sewers
unexpectedly.

"That wouldn't be a lot of fun, particularly if you're
in a two-foot drain. There's not much room for you
and too much water in a two-foot drain. There is the
danger of being rinsed out of a sewer. But that's what
makes it such a great adventure. That's the fear that
attracts me. It would be like the opening scene in
'Raiders of the Lost Ark'; except instead of a big
concrete ball hurtling down the tube, there'd be a
wall of water to wash skinny little Paul out into the
river. We have to be right out of our minds in order
to go into a regular cave. We're looking for danger.
If it were safe I wouldn't even bother going. You may
as well sit on a park bench."

We clambered back down the sewer and went home to
someone's house for a beer. Everyone changed out of
their wet clothes, and I listened to caving stories late into
the night.

"You'll come with us?" they asked, "Next spring. We'll
take you to Tennessee and show you a real squeeze."

"Sure," I said, "Sure."

KING OF THE PAPERBOYS

I have arranged to meet Martin Gorman several hours before dawn on a chilly January morning. We have agreed to meet at his house so I can join him on his paper route.

Martin is a paperboy. He got his first route delivering the *Globe and Mail* when he was nine years old. That was a long time ago. Twenty-three years ago, to be exact. Martin is still delivering the same paper to the same houses every morning. I am about to go to work with the Gordie Howe of paperboys.

Martin is dressed and waiting for me on his front porch when I arrive. He looks like he is about to go jogging. He is wearing a pair of loose-fitting pants, a sweater, a sweatshirt and sneakers.

"Hi. I'm Martin," he says, glancing at his watch. "We have to get going, or we are going to be late."

We get into his car and set off to pick up his papers. Martin has three hundred. He has to begin every morning at five-thirty if he is going to be finished by the 7 A.M.

deadline his paper promises for home delivery. Three hundred papers in an hour and a half works out to twenty seconds a paper. That includes picking them up at the corner, opening them, folding them, moving from place to place and executing the delivery. I look at my watch and wonder if we will make it. Martin looks over and smiles.

"I work fast," he says.

Yes, indeed.

Our first stop is a high-rise complex not far from Martin's house. Martin has several high-rises on his route. He likes the high-rises because he can move through them quickly. They weren't here twenty-three years ago when he started delivering papers.

We pull into the parking lot and Martin explodes out of the car, turning to haul a seventy-pound stack of newspapers out of the back. He heaves the bundle on top of his shoulders and jogs towards the building carrying the papers like a native bearer in a 1940s adventure movie. As I stumble along behind him, he explains that it is a waste of time to stuff papers into a bag.

In the elevator Martin pushes three buttons with three quick jabs. He wants to stop on the tenth, fifteenth and twentieth floors. Each time the elevator door opens, Martin throws a bundle of papers out. We ride all the way to the top.

Then we start down by foot.

Martin gallops through the building like a possessed man trying to hand-plant a huge field of corn. He runs the length of each floor slapping papers down, headline up, at door after door. At the end of each floor he tumbles down the stairs to the floor below. When we hit the fifteenth floor, he picks up the pile of papers he threw out of the elevator on the way up and keeps going. Down. Down. Down. He moves like a whirling dervish. We do the twenty floors in twelve minutes flat. About thirty-six seconds a floor. And that includes the ride up in the elevator. Every door on every floor looks exactly the same. As we fly through the building, I wonder how Martin remembers which doors are supposed to get a paper.

If letter carriers moved like Martin, walking on the sidewalks would be hazardous during the day. We would be able to do away with Special Delivery and get rid of Priority Post.

Back in the car, we are spinning along St. Clair towards the next area. Using a car may not be completely fair, but if Gordie Howe can use his elbows, I decide it's OK for Martin to use his automobile. Every morning, Martin loads his car and uses it to get from one section of his route to the next. As we drive through the darkness, Martin suddenly stops, and something wonderful happens.

We are stopped in front of what is either an office tower or an exclusive apartment complex. Whatever it is, the building is shut up tight. Mysteriously, a security guard appears at the front door and opens it, throwing a crack of light into the gloomy street. Standing beside his car, Martin draws his arm back and throws a paper towards the barely opened door.

The universe stops to watch what happens next. It is like a moment frozen in time. Because Martin doesn't just throw the paper, he . . . *launches* it. It rises over the car, climbs above the sidewalk, sails over the snowbank and then hangs over the lawn like a softball hanging over centre field on a summer night. Then, magically, the paper arcs down towards the door and – as I watch with my jaw hanging open – slides through the crack and slaps down at the feet of the guard. Martin smiles. I think I see the guard shrug, but I'll never be sure. We are a block away before he could have stooped down to pick the paper up.

Martin says he likes to throw newspapers.

"Probably early on I couldn't throw papers as well as I can throw them now. The accuracy comes with age. Now I can pretty well hit a door from centre street and not have to go too much further, which is a help in the snow, because otherwise you'd have to go over snow banks in the middle of the street. When you throw a paper from the street you have to make sure that it stays folded when it lands. That's very important, because if it doesn't stay folded then there's a chance of it blowing away. Sometimes you can get great throws. I think it has happened more than once, but not very often, when you can throw a paper from the centre of the street and it doesn't just land on the person's veranda, but actually lands on the one step up to the doorway, so when they open their door it's sitting right on the upper step, right by the door. That's a hard throw to make. I like to play golf, and when I make a throw like that it's just like having a wedge shot land at the pin."

Martin started delivering papers because he needed an allowance that he could rely on. Both his mother and father worked in the theatre, and allowance money wasn't always available. These days he works as a high school teacher during the day, but he still delivers papers for the money. He calls it enterprising jogging and figures that he makes between $6,000 and $7,000 a year. He uses the money for vacations. Every year he goes golfing in Bermuda. Martin says you can do all right delivering papers.

"It's not unheard of for some people to actually make a living at it. There are some men and women in the city who do four or five or six hundred *Globe and Mail*s every morning. Combine that with perhaps the same number of papers in the afternoon, and you could make $20,000 to $25,000 a year. For someone who is doing a route of a hundred papers, it would be somewhere in the neighbourhood of $40 a week or so. And a hundred papers would only take about an hour each day."

The job isn't without its difficult moments. Saturdays are never easy. Martin says Saturday's paper is always heavy, and because of the TV insert, impossible to fold. He says that rain can make a mess of his morning, but that his most disturbing problem is dealing with neighbours who steal each others' newspapers. He says this usually happens on Saturday mornings in large apartment buildings, when someone wakes up early, sees that it is snowing out, wants a morning paper and spots one lying in the hallway. Of course, the paperboy gets blamed for forgetting to deliver the missing paper. Having lived with the problem for too many years, Martin has devised an action plan he invokes whenever he is confronted with a repeating theft. He devised his plan with one of his customers who had lost her paper for several weeks running.

"I suggested that she tape a little piece of string to the underside of her paper and have the string go right under her door. So when she sees the string moving, she quickly opens the door and she finds out who it is that has been taking the paper. Well, this one customer did that, and when she opened the door a very embarrassed man said, 'Oh, I'm sorry, I was just checking the headline. I wanted to see what was happening.' But she knew she had caught the

person who had been taking her paper, and of course
it didn't happen after that."

There is a wonderful secret world in a big city before the
sun comes up. In the hours before dawn, cities turn into
villages. It is a world that belongs to breadmen, post
office workers, the odd cab driver and paperboys. At
seven o'clock suddenly the cars come out and the village
turns into a city again.

It is a strange sensation roaming through that early
morning with Martin and his papers. It feels like we are
doing something important. The headlines seem powerful
and potent, and as we drop each paper on each doorstep,
I feel personally responsible for delivering the NEWS.

Then at seven o'clock, the sun washes the secret away
and the cars clog the streets and Martin's day as a
paperboy is almost over. But there is one more ritual to
perform before he becomes a grown-up again. Every
morning when he has delivered his last paper, Martin
does what he had done since he was nine years old.
He goes to The Rail Coffee Shop for toast and orange
juice. Martin may be a grown man today, but to Louie
Papadakos, who has been serving him for twenty-three
years, he is still a kid.

"I never call him 'Martin,' myself; always I call him
'son.' He grew up with me. He was a little kid, now
he's grown up and he's big, but I still call him son.
Different people they come here and they say,
'Louie, his name is Martin,' and I say, I know, but
always I call him son. Did you notice when he walked
in this morning that he walked right behind the
counter and poured himself his own glass of water
and his own orange juice? He does that all the time.
You'll never see another customer do that. No one
else goes behind the counter; he's the only one who

does it. Sometimes on his way out he picks up his own change there. He leaves two dollars and he picks up his change and he goes. Nobody checks him, nobody looks at it. And you know, every day he gives us a free paper in here, yes, always he leaves a paper in here. He's got some extra, you know, and he leaves it for us."

Martin and I sit in a booth in Louie's coffee shop together. He drinks his orange juice, looks at his watch and says he has to go. He doesn't want to be late for school. I say I'll stay and have another coffee. He gives me a paper. "It's an extra," he says. I sit in the booth and watch as he goes up to the cash register and leaves his money on the counter. No one comes to check him.

Everyone should have a restaurant where they are allowed behind the counter, I think as I pick up my paper and flip to the sports section.

MEMORIES OF THE MILKMAN

Another thing wrong with the world today is that people just don't look the way they are supposed to anymore. Bank tellers look like they have popped into work on their way to a disco; doctors like they are on their way to someone's cottage. Hockey players and cops all look like kids. I find this disturbing. And that's why it felt so good to meet Al Barrett.

Al is a milkman. Quite frankly I didn't know we had milkmen anymore, but there are still a handful of guys out there delivering milk door to door, and Al Barrett is one of them. He has been a milkman for twenty-four years. For the past fifteen years he has had the same route.

I met Al one morning in a parking lot before dawn. We had arranged to meet so I could spend a day in his truck while he delivered milk. As I have already said, Al was looking good. By that I mean he was old enough and dressed just right to be a milkman. He was wearing dark-blue pants, a light-blue shirt, and a windbreaker with "Al" stitched up over the chest pocket. Around his waist he had a money belt filled with change, so he jingled as he walked. The crowning touch, though, was the cardigan he had on under his windbreaker. The cardigan was about four inches longer than his jacket, so it hung out the bottom just the right amount. Al was dressed both with an eye to his occupation and an eye to the winter sky. He smiled at my appraisal.

"You wear your boots, you know, your underclothes and your long johns and that. And if you want, you've got your gloves and your cap. All the caps have earmuffs in case you need them. But I don't think I've had my earmuffs down in the last two years."

Not only was Al dressed right, everything about him was right. Starting with his truck. It had a familiar sour smell peculiar to the milk trucks of my youth. I had forgotten about that smell, and you probably have, too, but it would come back to you if you could step into Al's truck for a minute. In the back he had jugs of milk and cartons of eggs and tubs of cottage cheese and butter and yoghurt. In the front, on the dash, he had an appropriate collection of junk, including a block of wood about a foot long, into which he had drilled two holes just the right size to hold the two cups of coffee that were steaming up the windshield when I clambered in.

"Coffee?" he said, gesturing to the dash. It was the first word he said to me as I swung into his truck.

The block of wood keeps the coffee from spilling as Al drives around his neighbourhood. He drives twenty-five miles a day, which he says is not too bad. He says that he knows some guys who have to do over a hundred miles. He says he is lucky because his route begins close to the dairy.

He looked at his watch and asked me if I was ready.

"I don't like to be late. I keep my time within ten, fifteen minutes of hitting a customer day by day. If I'm over fifteen minutes late they usually figure I've got a flat tire or I've got into problems with the truck or something. I leave the dairy at seven and the first call knows I'm there by five past seven. If she wants anything extra, bang she's at the door, or she leaves a note."

Al got all sorts of notes as he jogged from house to house. Some were casual and offhand. We found one someone had printed quickly on a piece of paper towel that said, "Two creams, Al." Someone else used the back of an envelope that had once been addressed simply to "Mom and Dad". Other notes were obviously meant to be more permanent – keepers that Al returned to the milk box. These belonged to thoughtful people who just had to reach into the cupboard for the note they needed every morning – carefully lettered notes on pieces of cardboard that said things like "Orange juice with pulp". Some notes Al crumpled up and tossed into a cardboard box in the front of his truck. Still others he saved in a special book or on a clothes-peg that was stuck within reach of his door. The savers, and there weren't many, were from customers who have, at some time or another, disputed what they owed when Al comes on Saturdays to settle accounts.

As we lurched from house to house, Al and I began to reminisce about the milk business. When I was a boy, milk used to come by horse. The Guaranteed Pure Milk Company sent orange wagons from door to door. The horses had oat bags strapped to their snouts and knew the houses where they were expected to stop and wait. The milkman ran up the driveway carrying a wire basket with six chattering glass bottles of milk.

Al never used a horse, but he remembers the "stand-up

trucks". These were trucks designed to be driven standing up. The seats folded away and tucked under the dash. There was one pedal to the left of the accelerator that did double duty as a clutch and a brake. If you pushed the pedal halfway down it worked as a clutch; all the way to the floor changed it to a brake.

"You didn't want to take corners too fast in a stand-up truck," said Al, "or you'd end up swinging out the door and hanging on the steering wheel for dear life."

Of course we started to talk about the glass milk bottles. And of course I started to lament their passing, which is where Al and I parted company, because he wasn't the least bit sorry to see the end of them.

"You used to cut your fingers a lot on the bottles for one thing. Because at that time we used to pick up three bottles in our fingers. If they had sharp edges on them you would cut the inside of your fingers. Everything was cold, especially in the winter-time, and your bottles froze quicker than cartons do. You would have an awful mess in your truck from all the cream popping over the top. And cracked bottles. A lot of the time when it was real cold I have seen the milk freeze right in the bottles, and the bottles would split. And then you just had to return the milk to the dairy as a lost cause."

Now from a milkman's perspective that all might make sense, but I remember how the cone of frozen cream used to rise out of the top of our milk bottles like the space shuttle, and I remember that frozen cream told me a lot more about the weather than anything the weather man ever said. It was something you could believe. Cream never lied.

We used to buy strips of red tickets from our milkman that you would fold carefully into the mouth of the bottle.

The idea was not to let them fall all the way in. Later they brought out round ones with holes in the middle that fit right in the top. Everyone thought they were very modern. Very downtown. I remember missing the old square red ones. However, all the milkmen liked the new ones because they hated digging milk tickets out of the bottom of milk bottles. Especially in the winter.

> "We used to carry a small stick with us because the tickets would freeze in there. So you would thaw them out, or thaw out the ice in the bottom of the milk bottle and get this stick and dig out the tickets because they got all wet down there. We used to bang the bottles on the truck. Sometimes the ticket would fall out, but a lot of times it would just stick there. And you just couldn't work it up unless you had a little stick to poke into the milk bottle."

I asked Al if there was anything he missed from the old days. He ran his hand through his hair and said that he missed the competition. There is only one dairy left in our town that delivers milk from door to door. Al remembers the days when each neighbourhood had three or four milkmen competing for business. Today just about everyone buys their milk from the corner store, and the edge is gone from the business. In those days it was a dog-eat-dog world, and any time someone new moved into a neighbourhood, all the guys would fight for the new customer.

> "We would run up there, and everyone would try and beat each other up the street to try to pick up the new customer. Or you would leave them a free quart of milk, which was called a promotion. You would knock on the door, and if no one was at home you would leave it there between the doors or something. Some days you would go by and you would see four

different quarts of milk sitting up there because
everyone had left a quart of milk for the new people.
It was strictly up to themselves who they took from.
In time, you know, I don't think there'll be any
milkmen on the road. Some kids are growing up and
they don't even know what a milkman is. They just
think you go to the store to buy milk. They've never
seen a milkman."

Al may be part of a dying breed, but he still cares about
what he does. Every time he left a dozen eggs in
someone's milk box, he opened it first and checked each
egg carefully.

"If you don't do that," he said, "you can leave someone
a cracked egg."

He also cares about his customers. He took a vacation
last summer for the first time in fifteen years. He took his
family to Niagara Falls. His family kept telling him to walk
slower. He was used to walking fast, you see, when he
delivered milk. So he slowed down and then his legs
started to cramp up because they weren't used to moving
so slow. When he finally got back to work, he told
everyone that he'd had a good time, but secretly he was
glad it was over. He missed his people. And I can
understand that, because after only a day I had already
begun to develop my favourite customers.

There was 50 Boel. A woman who took the works. Most
people took a few quarts of milk, but the woman at 50
Boel took sour cream, butter, a quart of table cream,
cottage cheese and the milk.

"She does that every week," smiled Al proudly.

There was also the woman at 8 Maplewood who signals
Al if she wants him to drop in by leaving her milk box
slightly ajar.

"I guess she wants something today," said Al, peering
into the dawn as we cruised by her house.

There was the deaf man who had his doorbell fixed so when you press it all the lights in his house start flashing.

And there were the two families that had given Al side door keys so he could let himself in and put the milk right into the fridge. Neither of these families left notes. Al just looked in the fridge and knew what they needed.

This all struck me as rather nice. Al seemed to agree.

"As far as I'm concerned it's a healthy life. You're out in all kinds of weather, of course, but I think it's healthier than being stuck in a factory or an office. At least you are breathing fresh air."

"You've got a fifteen-year-old kid," I asked. "Do you want him to be a milkman?"

"No, I don't," said Al quickly. "I hope he goes a lot further than that. I mean, there's a lot easier jobs for one thing, and well, he's very smart and I think he can get up higher in the business world, maybe in computers or something like that."

"What if he said he wanted to be a milkman?" I asked again. "What would you say then?"

"I don't know what I would say to him," said Al. "I would try to talk him out of it. I would just say there isn't any future in the milk business. Unless you own a big dairy or something, I guess, then there could be a future in it."

On Fridays Al spends an hour in the lobby of an old people's home. He parks his truck and lugs in a couple of cartons of milk and eggs and butter and sets up a table by the elevator. Like everyone else on his route, the people at the home can buy their milk cheaper at the corner store. But they enjoy it when Al comes, and there are always plenty of customers on hand. They, too, remember with fondness the days when neighbourhood windows all across town were festooned with signs that said MILK PLEASE or NO MILK TODAY.

But those days are gone. Back then Al used to work until four in the afternoon. These days, likely as not, he is finished for the day by lunch. There is just not enough business anymore for a full day's work. Not that Al is complaining.

"You put in an average of six hours a day at the most, which is nice. You start early in the morning and you finish early enough so you have all your afternoon. I get home, and if there's a snowfall I have my driveway cleaned. I'm usually the first on the street to have it cleaned. It works out all right in that way. In the summer I love working in the garden. My wife and I spend a lot of hours working in the garden. I have a fair-sized vegetable patch. And she has all her flowers and her roses and that. We keep ourselves busy. If not, if it's a real hot day, then we go over and see the neighbour and have a swim in their pool."

About half of Al's customers like him to knock on their door as he goes by. They want more than a quart of milk from their milkman. They want a chat, an opinion, a story and maybe a question about their family. The thing about those houses is that Al hardly ever has to ring the bell. Those customers always seem to be there, by the door, ready. As if they have waited all morning for him to arrive. Al said they don't have to do that. He said they just get used to him.

"They know when I'm supposed to come," he says, "and I try to be regular enough so they can set their watch by me."

I wish I could.

Here's to Al Barrett. And any other working milkman you might know.

HOW NOW BROWN COW?

This is my Bovine Polemic. It is a biased, slanted, prejudiced presentation about a cow. Not a particular cow, but an entire breed. I am about to jettison any sense of neutrality or even-handedness that you might expect from a responsible journalist. Herewith I fling fairness out the window. I want to glorify, celebrate, eulogize and flatter . . . the Jersey cow.

She used to be everyone's favourite. There was a time when a traveller who felt compelled to count cows as she whisked across Canada would, at day's end, note that her tally contained more brown ones than anything else. Today, of all the cows that we milk from coast to coast, 90 to 95 percent of them are Holsteins. Holsteins are the hip ones – the black-and-white ones that everyone is wearing on their sweatshirts, and has hanging on their walls, and has plastered on the covers of their magazines and, most important, has standing in their barns. Both rural and urban Canadians have abandoned the Jersey cow.

Not without reason.

Over the past forty-five years, genetic engineers have

mounted relentless breeding programs using black-and-white cows. Given their terms of reference, these programs have been wildly successful. The geneticists have created a virtual four-legged milk machine – a machine that converts feed into huge volumes of milk low in butterfat. Which, of course, is the kind of milk everybody wants these days. No breed is better built to milk than these designer cows. They have, for example, been deliberately constructed with more space underneath for their udders. The latest frontier is to make them bigger overall. Some geneticists predict that they'll soon turn out Holsteins as big as elephants. And wait, they say, till you see the amount of milk we'll get from those suckers. We have all been brainwashed into believing that this is something we should be happy about. That somehow the Holstein is the answer to all of our problems.

Someone has to stand up for the Jersey.

There are both emotional and sensible arguments for holding on to brown cows. Both facts and feelings. I have loaded up both cannons. I am going to start with the feelings.

There would be no Jerseys in Canada today if it wasn't for a handful of stubborn farmers who didn't dump their Jersey herds along with everyone else in the mad rush to switch to Holsteins. These farmers who stood by the Jersey have had to put up with a lot of abuse for their loyalty. For one thing, they get teased at farmer parties. Ask anyone who grew up on a farm what it was like when Dad milked cows that were different from everyone else's. Neighbours would tut-tut and cluck that those were the folks who were too poor to milk Holsteins but too proud to milk goats.

No one bothered to mention that Jerseys happen to be the world's most beautiful cows. And why shouldn't aesthetics count in the barnyard? The Jersey is a solid, stocky, well-muscled animal. Not all sharp and angular.

And she is warmly coloured, washed with friendly, romantic earth colours. She is tawny, fawn, amber, auburn, nutty and dusty. And that's not all. Jerseys have big brown dewy deer eyes. Beautiful big brown deer eyes. And well-formed, almost elegant muzzles. This in place of the sloppy, dripping cow lips you've grown used to.

Not only are Jerseys prettier, they are smarter. Albert Taylor should know. He has a whole barn full of them.

"Jerseys are extremely inquisitive creatures. If you have a sick cow on the field and you have to get the vet to come and have a look, the rest of the herd will crowd around you wondering what in the world is going on. If you do the same thing in a field of cows of other breeds, they just continue to go about their business eating grass. Not only are Jerseys inquisitive, they're also extremely smart. Our cows all learned their own stalls within five or six days without any further help, so I think that indicates a few brains, anyway."

I spent a day in Albert Taylor's barn and saw just how smart his cows are. I watched them waiting patiently outside while he mucked out their stalls. Then watched while they lined up politely to get back in. They lined up the way people line up to get into a hockey game. Except when Albert threw open the barn door the whole herd found their places without ushers. And they all got it right. Each cow found her own stall. Except for one who stood in front of her slot without stepping in. Albert shuffled his feet and looked away.

"She's a little eccentric," he said, slipping a rope over her neck. "She won't go into the stall unless I put a rope on her."

Sure enough, once Albert had slipped a rope around her neck, she slipped into position with no further fuss. It seems she fell down one evening stepping over the automatic stable cleaner and the rope is her security blanket.

Now, anyone who has tried to stuff a Holstein into a stall (and I worked on a dairy farm for two summers, so I know what I am talking about) knows that Holsteins are big cows. If they don't want to go somewhere, and you lean against them, they can lean you into the middle of next week. Jerseys are smaller than Holsteins and, if push comes to shove, easier to move around.

And that's not all. Albert has been milking his herd of Jerseys for over twenty-five years. In that time he has never had to get up in the middle of the night to help one of his cows calve. Because Jerseys are smaller, their calves are smaller. Find me someone who works with Holsteins who can say the same thing.

I have been trying, for a while, to marshal all the emotional arguments as to why we should stand by the Jersey cow – the beautiful but brilliant underdog, the easy-going cow with the pleasant disposition. It is time to put sentiment aside and lay out the facts.

First off, I concede that there is no other cow in the world that gives more milk than a Holstein. I also concede that because she is bigger, a butcher will pay more for her when she is finished as a milker. There is just more of her, and because 35 percent of our beef comes from old dairy cows, this is an important economic consideration. I concede both points without an argument. If you choose to milk Holsteins, you'll get more milk from each cow and pocket more money at the end of the road when it is time to trade her in.

But let's talk quality. Think back to the days when you could go to the store and buy a quart of Jersey milk. It was so good, you had to pay a premium for it. But in each glass you got more butterfat, more protein, more milk solids, more carotene and more calcium. Albert Taylor's partner and brother, Gordon, remembers drinking Jersey milk when he was a kid. Each glass of milk, he says, was rich and smooth going down.

> "You can just picture it. It reminds me of a real thick milkshake, except you're dealing with the original. Not milk with ice cream added. Jersey milk is rich and it's creamy and – oh, boy, it sounds like a beer commercial, doesn't it. But it is, it's just delicious."

Cheesemakers know how rich Jersey milk is. A cheese-maker will tell you that if he can get his hands on pure Jersey milk, he can make 20 percent more cheese than he could with the same amount of "normal" milk. You just have to look at Jersey milk to know it is different. Instead of that sort of sickly blue hue we have gotten used to, Jersey milk is a rich, nearly yellow colour. It looks like French vanilla ice cream.

But let's get down to the nitty gritty. No one disputes that cow to cow, a Holstein will make more money than a Jersey. It has, however, been suggested that farm to farm, a Jersey operation will be more profitable than a barn of Holsteins. There are two reasons why.

First, because it is richer, in many parts of Canada a farmer can get a premium for Jersey milk – as much as 15 to 20 percent more per litre. That means he doesn't have to sell as much milk to have as much money in his milk cheque. This is important because in Canada you have to buy milk quotas. If you want to produce a quart of milk a day, you have to pay for that right. So if you can get more income for less milk, then you can buy less quota and consequently keep your expenses down. That's number one. More money for less milk.

Second, because Jerseys are smaller than Holsteins, they eat less. Because they eat less, expenses go down again. You don't have to grow as much feed. So you don't have to farm as many acres.

Put these facts together and you find that your debt load, and therefore your interest payments, will be lower. Consequently your profitability will increase.

And that is why (and here comes the good news) the Jersey cow, which had almost disappeared from Canadian pastures in 1977, seems to have begun a tentative and almost imperceptible resurgence. According to Peter Doswell, editor of *Canadian Jersey Breeder* magazine, Jersey milk is now available on the market in British Columbia, and all-Jersey cheese is being made in Alberta and Quebec.

> "One company that is doing well with Jersey milk in British Columbia is even having Jersey milk flown from British Columbia to Ontario to do some test marketing. So there are indications that maybe – I didn't think it would happen in my lifetime, but maybe – Jersey milk is going to be back on the market as Jersey milk and not part of a whole pool of mixed-up stuff. We shouldn't really be surprised, I guess, because quality, just like the cream on Jersey milk, will always float to the top."

Now, all of this is actually important. The incredible popularity of the Holstein has hurt more than just the Jersey cow. Entire breeds of cows have been dropping by the wayside. Have you seen any Guernseys or Milking Shorthorns lately? If things keep going like this, it is possible, fifty years from now, that we could have only Holsteins left. And that is very troubling to some people.

Scientists have been so busy trying to develop the perfect cow, that the bloodlines from as few as twenty bulls could dominate most of the dairy cattle around the world within, say, twenty years. What the breeders are forgetting is that things tend to change rapidly these days. They could create a superbreed of cows that works today (which means cows that produce huge volumes of low-fat milk), and find that breed obsolete fifty years from now when the demand might change to high-protein milk. And if that happens, we would be in trouble. That is why we have to keep genetic material around that might be needed. We have to nurture animals that might not have an obvious market value today.

So here's to the Jersey farmers who have been plugging along for the last decade. I, for one, think the trend is changing. I predict that there will be a lot more Jerseys around in the next few years, and I hope all those farmers who stuck with them get rich.

A DRIVE IN THE COUNTRY

When I was a university student, I worked several summers on a small dairy farm in St. Eugene, Ontario. I worked for a man named Bill Smith who owned about one hundred acres and milked about twenty cows. I was the hired hand – the "man", as he used to call me. "Now we got a man, Ma," I remember him saying the morning I arrived, "We'll shoot over to the church and cut the lawn before we start in the fields." We loaded two lawn-mowers into the back of his pick-up truck and bumped over to the church, but when we got there, the grass had already been cut. Someone else had beaten us to it. I think Bill paid me five dollars a day plus room and board. I didn't get rich those summers, but I ate well, developed a love of the family farm and learned a lot about community commitment, hard work and family.

I thought of the Smiths and those summer mornings as I read the letter from Elisabeth Hietkamp. She had written to me at "Morningside" from *her* farm in Palmerston, Ontario.

Dear Stuart:
It is early in the morning, just past five. The countryside is
starting to wake up. The birds are throwing a gorgeous
concert through my open window, through which I can see
a ripe moon hanging over the garden fence. Pretty soon I
have to reload my van and start on my daily rounds. That
is what I want to tell you about. I am a farm wife. But we
are one of those farm families who haven't made it. We
had to sell our dairy herd and our quota. And, like about
80 percent of the farm wives in this country, I had to get a
job off the farm in order to maintain the cash flow. But I
am in my fifties and the scarce jobs in this area seem to
always go to the young and pretty women. A couple of
years ago, in desperation, I started my own business. I am
a pedlar. Every day I travel along the dirt roads from farm
to farm in my van selling work clothes, jeans, gloves,
overalls and other things you need when you work in the
country. I visit thirty to forty different farms a day. . . .

I received the letter in May, just before "Morningside"
ended for the summer. In it, Elisabeth went on to invite
me to spend a day with her, travelling in her van from
farm to farm.

It was a chilly November evening six months later when I
finally pulled up to the Hietkamps' farmhouse. The plan
was for me to sleep on the farm that night so I would be
ready to go out with Elisabeth early the next morning.

Elisabeth and her husband were waiting for me inside,
reading the local newspaper by the woodstove. I would
guess they were both in their mid-fifties. He looked like a
prosperous dairy farmer. She looked like George Bush's
wife. Her elegant blue-grey hair almost shone. You could,
I thought, take her off the farm and put her in a big city
boardroom, and she would fit right in.

Though it was late, we sat for some time by the hissing

stove. At first we talked awkwardly, the way people do when they first meet. Then we fell comfortably silent and listened as the wood smoke wisped up the chimney, danced across the farm fields and disappeared into the starry sky. We sat like a family sits. And after we had sat for some time, Elisabeth suddenly began to talk about how she and her husband had lost their farm. A barn had burned, she said, then their entire herd of cattle had got sick and had to be put down, interest rates were high, you can't just bounce back, and then one day there was a letter from the bank and it was all over. Her husband stared intently at the fire as she talked.

Elisabeth knew she had to get a job off the farm but, as she had written, this was easier said than done. When she had the idea of selling farm clothes door to door, it seemed like something that might work. But she didn't have any money to get the business off the ground. She needed a loan. She soon found herself sitting across a desk from the same bank manager who was closing in on her farm loans. She had to talk him into lending her more money.

"I went to the banker and said I had an idea but I would need to invest about ten thousand dollars altogether to get going. We laid out a budget. I needed about five, six thousand dollars worth of stock. I also needed money for a van. Well, to make a long story short, he gave me the money, and off I went."

We were up the next morning with the rooster, and after a hearty farm breakfast, Elisabeth prepared her van for our day on the road. It was so crammed with clothes, it looked like someone had emptied out an Eaton's basement, put it through a compactor and then shoehorned the entire mess into the back of the van. There were hundreds of plaid farm shirts swinging on a pole that ran from the front of the van to the back. And there were jeans piled on shelves, and gloves and socks and table-cloths and all sorts of odds and ends tucked into home-made cubby-holes. Elisabeth explained that after four years on the road, she could afford to carry about $10,000 worth of inventory with her.

We clambered into the van and set off under a chilly grey sky that was threatening snow. We spun down the highway and past the Campbell soup factory.

"A lot of farm women work there," said Elisabeth, pointing. "I hope I never have to. It would be like a prison sentence."

We bumped off the highway onto the dirt roads and back into farm country. We passed men out in the fields who were hurrying to finish their ploughing before the snow came, and saw seagulls following the tractors as if the tractors were tugboats. The seagulls were looking for worms in the freshly turned soil. Some of the roads we went down seemed more like laneways than roads, and we had to navigate around big wet clumps of dirt that had fallen off the ploughs and lay in the roadway like dead animals.

We drove for nearly an hour before we reached the concession where Elisabeth was going to work that day. It was nine-thirty when we pulled into the first farmyard. A woman came out from the kitchen, with a big smile. She wanted to tell us how happy she was to see the van.

"It's the lady with the jeans. I've been waiting for her."

"That's what you call her?" I asked.

"That's what we call her. The lady with the jeans. I don't know her name. I know she's Dutch. I'm really glad she came today."

While I stood by the edge of the truck, and her twins churned around the yard on their trikes, the women rummaged through the back of the van and came up with some socks, some underwear and, almost triumphantly, two pairs of jeans for her husband.

"Last night my husband told me to do some mending. He set two pairs of jeans aside and said please mend these today, so I put them in the washing machine. I was hoping maybe you would come along so I could pitch them in the garbage, because they're beyond repair. There's only so much you can do to jeans."

She paid for her clothes, and we waved a jaunty goodbye as we pulled out of the yard. Driving towards the next farm, Elisabeth told me that door-to-door selling in farm country has a long tradition. She told me about the merchants who used to come to her farm peddling everything from lightbulbs and spices to frozen fish and insurance. Then she said that as far as she knew, she was the only person left on the road near Palmerston.

As we bounced along the road, I began to realize why. We didn't sell anything at the next eleven farms. At many of them, no one was home. We would drive down the lane, get barked at, calm the dog down, knock on the door, then head down the road to the next lane and the next dog. Whenever we did find someone home, it seemed they had just been to town and bought their winter stuff. We went at it for about two hours with no luck, when Elisabeth finally pulled the van over to the side of the road, sighed and opened an apple juice.

"This is depressing," I said.

She shrugged and said she used to find it depressing, too, but not any longer.

"In the early days I would feel like turning around and going home a couple of times a day. Of course, you can't do that because there's always the possibility that the next farm will be the best sale that day."

"I shouldn't have said depressed," I confessed. "I'm not feeling depressed. If I was really being honest, I'm a little bit embarrassed that we haven't . . . embarrassed for you, that no one's buying stuff. Should I be embarrassed?"

"No," said Elisabeth. "That's business. It's very depressing if you don't sell, but you have to keep on going."

"So on we go?" I asked.

"Well, if you stay at home you're sure you won't sell anything, right?"

As if to prove Elisabeth's point, it looked like we were about to strike pay dirt at the next farm. Before we stopped for juice, we had hit five farms in a row where no one was home. When we pulled into the next yard, the kitchen door was open and a dog bounded out with its tail wagging. Here we go, I thought, as I sat in the van fiddling with my tape recorder. But by the time I had myself organized, Elisabeth was back in the car again.

"Nobody home here, either," she said.

Empty farmhouses, I suppose, were the overwhelming theme of the day. We stopped at over forty different farms and made sales at less than ten of them. Our best moment came near the end of the day.

It was cold in the van and I was freezing by the time we arrived at what would be our last farmhouse. The woman who met us at the door bought a pair of rubber boots and then said we should go out to the barn and find her husband. I was wearing long underwear and a T-shirt and a shirt and a sweater and a jacket, and I was still chilly, and therefore I was somewhat surprised, when we got to the barn, to find her husband wearing only a T-shirt and a light jacket. When he saw us, he wandered over and greeted us like it was the middle of summer.

"Did you get any stuff from these people here, Mother?" he asked his wife.

"Yeah, I got a pair of green boots like you did for the barn."

"Do you need a pair like that?" asked Elisabeth, the consummate salesperson.

"I've got them," he demurred, "and they sure keep your feet good and warm. How 'bout the work socks? How much are the work socks today?"

"Two-fifty," said Elisabeth, holding up a pair of grey socks. "Have you had these before?"

"No, but I know they're good and warm. But I have trouble because they go down on my feet. See what I do in the winter time is cheat a little, see. I wear two pairs of light socks. That seems to be the combination to keep my feet warm." He rummaged around in the open van and came up with some lighter socks. "And how much are these things?" he asked.

"Two seventy-five," said Elisabeth.

"Two seventy-five," he replied.

"Isn't that a good price?" asked Elisabeth.

"It is a good price," he decided.

After all the rejections we had experienced that day, and all the empty farms we had pulled into, it seemed as if this farmer and his wife had been put on earth just to make us feel good. His wife had bought the pair of boots for the barn, and he was going through the van as if it was his last chance to get clothes till spring.

"So we'll take two pair of these; better have a couple pair of these here. Do you think these will be worth a try?" he wondered, grabbing at some of the socks. "What the heck are these? They'd be good and warm, wouldn't they?"

"They are, yeah," said Elisabeth.

"Well, we'll take one pair of them. When you go to the auction sales you stand around a lot. You get cold." He looked at me shivering beside the van and added, "Just like the reporter here. He's getting cold as hell."

"She's gonna wait until I'm freezing and then sell me a pair of insulated coveralls," I said.

He turned to Elisabeth, smiling. "Hey, you know, when he's cold enough you can quote him any price you want. He'll pay."

"What do you farm?" I asked.

"Hog farming."

"How's the hog business?"

"Well, they tell us it's in for a little slide, but once Brian gets us into the Free Trade we'll be all right."

"All those Americans waiting for that Canadian bacon?" I asked.

"I think they're waiting for these hogs, so we're ready for them."

Elisabeth wrapped up the sale and we headed down the driveway, still cold, but feeling more cheery than we had for a while. When we reached the main road, Elisabeth pulled the van over and asked if I would drive. We switched places, she pointed me towards home and settled into the passenger seat with a calculator. As I drove, she flipped through her receipt book and started to work out her sales for the day.

"Four hundred dollars," she said after a while.

I looked out the window and saw that we were passing the Campbell soup factory again. I asked what profit she would get out of four hundred dollars of sales.

"About $140 profit," she replied.

Not bad, perhaps, but that was before expenses. We had put close to thirty dollars' worth of gas in the van that morning and now the gauge was showing low. If you factored in insurance and depreciation, that left less than one hundred dollars profit for the day. Which, Elisabeth said, was less than average. And, she added quickly, it seemed that she was getting more and more days like that.

"I really feel that business is going backward. The customers aren't there anymore. More and more farms are closing, and it has a real influence on my business. I don't know if my gross sales are down; I won't know till the beginning of the year. I don't have time to check it regularly. I haven't looked at any totals. But I feel it's down this year. I sure feel it's down."

It was dark when we got back to the farm. Elisabeth's husband was burning leaves on the front lawn. Their daughter, the last child still living at home, wasn't back from her after-school job. We went into the house and Elisabeth started peeling carrots for supper. As she worked, she looked out at her husband in the yard.

"It's hard on him since we sold the cows. He still has a few heifers that he is fattening for sale, and he still works the fields for the cash crop, but it is not the same as milking a full herd. All my husband likes to do is farm. That's what he wants to do. Farming is in his blood."

"Do you think he'll get a chance to do it again?" I asked.

"No," she said without hesitation.

"What about him? What does he think?" I asked.

"Oh, he gets tempted. When he sees a farm for sale, he says, 'I think I'm gonna borrow money and start milking again,' but it's just not realistic at our age to go into debt that far, no."

"What do you say to him when he says he wants to borrow money and do it all again?" I wondered.

"I say, 'Oh, Dad, you know better.' "

Elisabeth Hietkamp is no longer going door to door selling farm clothes. She has just begun selling cars for a Pontiac dealership in Palmerston, Ontario. She got the job soon after we spent our day together. But the van is still on the road. Elisabeth's husband, Gerrit, climbs behind the wheel these mornings. He has given up his dreams of getting his herd going again. At least, says Elisabeth, now that both she and her husband have jobs, it is likely they won't have to move off the farm altogether. The two incomes should make it possible for them to keep living at home. Their jobs also mean that the Hietkamps' farmhouse is empty all day. It has become another family farm with no one home to greet visiting pedlars.

HARDWARE STORES HAVE ALL THE ANSWERS

A good hardware store is a wonderfully old-fashioned institution. Going for hardware is like going for water at the village well. No matter when you go, there is always someone there with something to say, and sooner or later everyone you know drops by. But a hardware store is more than a meeting place. In an imperfect world, many hardware stores are quiet little corners of perfection – places to be both preserved and praised. This is my homage to hardware.

Why? Well, to begin with, hardware stores take note of the seasons. That used to be the role of pumpkins and professional sport, but you can't keep track of the seasons in the sports pages anymore. The Stanley Cup is sweated right into short-sleeve weather, and some baseball players open each season in stadiums where they are as likely to hit a snowball as a slowball. North American commerce has done its best to deny the rhythms of the natural world, but hardware stores acknowledge each changing season with elegant deliberation.

The weekend before you notice it is spring, the pile of snow shovels and toboggans on the sidewalk outside the hardware store is quietly replaced by . . . lawn mowers. On the shelf near the front of the store where they kept heaters all winter, suddenly you notice a precarious tower of picnic coolers. There are garden hoses coiled in the corner where they had humidifiers in January. There are lawn-care products on the shelf that used to hold the Christmas decorations.

Yes, clothing stores rotate their stock seasonally. But they do it with an eye to the next season. Hardware stores march lock-step with the natural world. They know where we are in time.

But that's not all. It is hardware stores who have held the line on shrink-wrap. The rearguard action against the plastic package is being fought in hardware stores across the country. You can still go to a hardware store and buy *one* nail, or *one* fuse. This, in a world where you must look long and hard to find a candy store where you can buy penny candy piece by piece. And when you buy your handful of nails, the man in the hardware store is going to weigh them (weigh them!) and slide them into a brown paper bag. Hardware stores haven't embraced plastic bags because nails go through plastic. As long as you can buy nails by the handful, there will be brown paper bags at hardware stores.

And brown paper bags are not the only constant. Hardware stores are a constellation of consistency. Where else can you get a jar of paste wax? Or a box of moth-balls? Or a can of Gillette 100 Percent Pure Lye Flakes, in a can sporting a gold lion?

Hardware stores break all the rules of modern mer- chandising. The store in my neighbourhood is not much bigger than the average living-room. Yet when they throw open their doors at 8:30 on Saturday morning, there are seven salesmen waiting to serve you. For the first two hours of most Saturday mornings, those seven clerks tag team each customer that comes in.

In a world where sales clerks are getting harder and harder to find, not only is my hardware store overstaffed, it is overstocked. As far as I can figure it, they have *everything* there. I had never even heard of Aero Powdered Dance Wax until I saw it on the shelf of my local store. It comes in a cardboard container, like the popular kitchen cleaners, with instructions that tell you to sprinkle the powder very lightly on the dance floor. "The feet of the dancers," says the can, "will produce the polish. It will not soil," it promises, "the most delicate fabrics." It also comes with the following cryptic warning: DO NOT USE TOO MUCH. Do they mean don't use it too often, or are they warning us that too much wax at one time might produce too much slidability and disastrous effects on the dance floor? What could go wrong or, more to the point, what *has* gone wrong on some faraway dance floor to make the manufacturers of Aero Powdered Dance Wax feel it prudent to tack on that warning? I assume the dance wax is meant for touch dancing. I didn't know anyone did that anymore. My hardware store has two cans of Aero Powdered Dance Wax.

But then, as I keep saying, they have everything. Tucked away on one side of the store are birdseed and bird feeders. Safely out of sight several aisles over, where it won't offend the birders, are tubes of Sannex Bird Repellent Paste, guaranteed to rid your life of sparrows, starlings, blackbirds and pigeons.

I have come across two major hotels in this country that do not insist on taking an imprint of my credit card when I check in. The last time I checked in, the working assumption at the Regina Inn and the Lord Elgin in Ottawa was that I'd drop by the front desk to settle my account on my way out. Hardware stores operate on the same principle. They are not festooned with convex mirrors bent on intimidating me. The cash register is almost universally at the back. Hardware stores operate on an act of faith, in a faithless age.

The most faithful stores, the secular equivalent of the great cathedrals of Europe – left their cash registers hidden on another floor altogether. The clerks in these holy places would take your money and insert it into a container that would, in turn, be placed in a vacuum tube and sucked away to where maybe God Himself made your change. Sadly, today, vacuum tubes are few and far between.

In a world of uncertainty, hardware stores stand out as islands of confidence. Theologians despair, psychiatrists and social workers shuffle their opinions as often as their feet, politicians shrug their numbed shoulders in despair, but the clerks in my hardware store field problems with the coolness of a left fielder in a grass outfield. No matter what your problems are, you should take them to the nearest hardware store.

Marty, at Wiener's hardware, says he has been asked everything. He flips open a notebook where he writes down his favourite questions. Things like the number of tomato seeds you must sow to harvest exactly ten pounds of tomatoes. Or where you can get some casket handles, please. Or if he has a self-cleaning lightbulb for an oven.

Hardware stores house a symphony of sounds. The paint-shaker thumping in the back of the store, the key-cutter grinding away, the newly sharpened clatter of someone's hand-pushed lawn-mower being wheeled to the front. (Is there a nicer sound in the world than a hand-pushed mower?) There is a radio on somewhere, not Muzak, and if all is right in the universe, maybe the radio has tubes.

My hardware store is about to pass to the third generation in the same family. Hy started the store in 1922. Gerry took it over from Hy. Marty, (Hy's grandson, Gerry's son) has a degree in microbiology. He had a job somewhere studying the mutation of the fruit fly. He left that to work in the hardware store.

The man has his head screwed on right.

MECCANO
METAPHYSICS

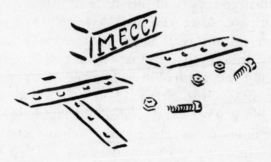

E d Barclay lives in a small house in a working-class
neighbourhood of Toronto. I have been told that Ed
has more Meccano in his basement than anyone else
in the world. Ed's not so sure. He knows of a chap in
Australia who has a large collection, and he has heard of a
few in England and the United States. But who knows.
Anyway, he says, looking shyly away, no one in Canada has
more Meccano than he does. He is sure of that.

Meccano is a building toy that is a memory of metal in a
world turned plastic. Today little boys snap plastic bricks
together into space towers and whirlybirds. When I was a
lad and basement-bound, my friends and I fumbled with
the red and green metal struts and the curious Meccano
screwdriver with the looped handle. Even back then the
structures we made seemed oddly antique. Everything we
assembled came out looking like the Eiffel Tower. Our
best attempts at modern architecture were strange shapes
that looked like they wanted to lumber back into the
Industrial Revolution.

Ed's Meccano room is at the back of the basement, and we have to bob our way under the furnace pipes to get there. Finally we are standing in front of the room that I have been told will take my breath away. Ed throws open the door and smiles. On cue I stop breathing.

There is probably enough Meccano in front of me to build a full-sized replica of the space shuttle and still have enough left over to erect a life-sized version of, well, the Eiffel Tower. And it is all neatly put away in thousands of tiny plastic drawers that wallpaper the entire room. Each drawer has been meticulously labelled. I open Drawer Q2 – Part 69A – Grub Screws 5-32″. It is indeed filled with tiny black screws. Ed smiles and hands me a black binder. It is his cross-referenced inventory control file. There are, he says, too many drawers to keep track of them by memory. When he needs a part, he uses the binder to lead him to the right drawer.

As well as the plastic drawers that cover the walls, there are three full-sized professional red metal machine cabinets stretched along one side of the room. The mechanic who works on my car might be able to fill one of these cabinets if he used all of his tools. Ed has filled all three with Meccano parts.

One night a few years ago, Ed calculated that he owned about two tons of Meccano. At the time he kept it upstairs in his den. He moved it all downstairs when he noticed that the den floor had begun to sag.

"When I went in the room I could feel a sort of bounce in the floor. So I phoned city hall. After going through about ten different departments I finally got someone who could tell me what the loading weights were for houses. And it's only fifty pounds per square foot, which is very small. I calculated the weight of the Meccano and the area of the floor it was on and realized that I was far exceeding the loading strains. So I had to load it all up and take it down to the basement and build my Meccano room down here on the concrete floor."

These days Ed is more worried about his age than he is about load bearings. Like most people still playing with Meccano, Ed is over fifty. A lot of his friends have given up the hobby recently. It's not that they are losing interest; it's just that the damn bolts are getting harder and harder to see. Ed picks up an official Meccano screwdriver and twirls it absent-mindedly on his finger.

"You know what Meccano is?" he asks. He doesn't want me to answer.

"It's a thrill in a box," he says.

I smile. He keeps talking.

"It's a thrill in a box. I can remember as a child the thrill of opening up a new box of Meccano. All those red and green parts. It's something you can create something with, something moving. You're the engineer in charge. If you build a locomotive you can be the engineer actually driving it. You can put the controls in the cab, work the throttle and make the engine go. Another time maybe you'll be a midway operator. I've made carousels that reached the ceiling, and you can sit there and operate it like you're actually at the midway operating the thing. You can make trucks with little gear boxes in them and you can put your fingers in and actually drive the truck."

When I was young all the boys I knew wanted a Meccano set at some point in their lives. But most of us who got one didn't go far with it. The letter "L" was about the most complicated thing I ever made. Like everyone, I knew a kid who had the steam engine and actually built mechanisms that moved. When I saw it with my own eyes I ran home and begged for a steam engine so I could make real stuff, too. Fortunately, cooler heads than mine prevailed. I never got the steam engine.

Ed worries that these are Meccano's last days. Even if you could buy it in toy stores, you can't interest kids in it anymore, he says. But if these are the dying days of a hallowed age, they are, by all accounts, good days.

Because all those kids who got the steam engine grew up, and through some sort of weird process of Darwinian selection, met each other. Now, as adults, they are egging each other on to bigger and better projects, and they are holding Meccano conventions, contests and shows, as well as trading information in the newsletters they write. Ed is part of a very active Meccano underground.

Upstairs, part of that underground is waiting for us. Ed's best friend, Colin Hoare, has dropped over for a drink. The three of us settle down in the living-room to talk about something I have never considered. The history of Meccano.

If you took a Popsicle stick, drilled seven holes along its length and painted it red, it would look just like a piece of Meccano. The elegance of the toy is its simplicity. The basic Meccano set has always consisted of three things: the metal struts, the screws and bolts, and the screwdriver. The challenge has always been to bolt the struts together in some sort of meaningful way.

Meccano was invented on a wet Saturday afternoon at the turn of the century by a British bookkeeper. Frank Hornby had been left to babysit his two sons. In an attempt to amuse them, he cut an old metal cookie tin into strips, cut some crude holes into the strips and set about with his boys to build something. Hornby and his sons had such a good time with his handiwork that it didn't take him long to realize he had come up with more than an afternoon's diversion. The rest, as they say, is history. Invented just before Queen Victoria died, Meccano was the perfect product for its time. It *was* the Industrial Revolution in a box. Britain was The Empire, and Meccano was the quintessential toy for empire builders.

Not only was it a great product for the times; Meccano had the good fortune to have been invented by a great salesman. Frank Hornby packaged his product in numbered sets. At the low end he began with a sad set that was actually identified by a big "0". But no matter where you started, you could always aspire to the fantastic extravagance rumoured to come with the top-of-the-line set Number 10. Number 10s came in an oak cabinet instead of a cardboard box. They were so expensive that very few were ever made. In 1955 a Number 10 set would have cost my dad $135. Today it is worth $3,000. ("I have seven Number 10s in my basement today," says Ed matter-of-factly.)

The steps between the sets were carefully devised so if you got Set 3 for your birthday, then for Christmas you'd ask for Set 3A, which would upgrade your 3 to a 4.

Hornby understood little boys. As well as playing on our compulsion to complete collections, he understood our urge to join groups. He established the Meccano Guild and brought out a monthly Meccano magazine. Once the Guild was going, he sent Meccano reps from one end of the Commonwealth to the other, and before long, enthusiasts everywhere were forming Meccano clubs. It was, says Ed's friend Colin, a brilliant marketing plan, the likes of which the toy business had never seen.

"The Meccano Magazine started up in 1916. It provided a means of communication for all the enthusiasts. Everybody would get the magazine on a monthly basis, there would be new instructions, there would perhaps be announcements of new parts, and they'd have new mechanisms for you to build. They used it as a communications system to let everybody know what was going on. They also built the Meccano Guild and established clubs, not only in the United Kingdom but throughout the world. In the thirties, Meccano really mushroomed. Everybody became enthusiastic. Lots of young boys would get their Meccano sets, and they would sign up and become members of the Meccano Guild. They'd send their sixpence to Meccano Limited and get their little certificate and badge declaring they were members of the Meccano Guild. It was an effective medium and an extremely popular toy."

Meccano was eventually killed by a number of things. After-school sports didn't help. Nor did television. Or Lego, or, for that matter, electronics. These days things are moved by chips, not by pulleys, chains and levers.

Though the company folded in Britain, Meccano sets are still being made in two countries – unreliably, in France (where they are produced sporadically by a licensee who has tried to add plastic parts to the product line) and, ironically, in Argentina, the site of Britain's last great imperial war.

Unfortunately, and, to purists like Colin and Ed, disturbingly, the Argentinians, while remaining true to Hornby's metal parts, have "modernized" the colours. Instead of the classic red and green, Argentinian Meccano is yellow and black.

Allan Bedford, who lives in London, Ontario, has constructed a special kiln and uses home-made paint bombs to wipe out this Argentinian revisionism. He restores and repaints Argentinian parts to their more traditional red and green.

There are other unsung heroes in the struggle to keep

Meccano alive. Giuseppe Servetti, an Italian, was the first to manufacture replicas of hard-to-find parts. One of the rarest parts is a machine that never came with a set. The miniature circular saw that actually worked was sold for a few years as an add-on part. It was known, says Colin Hoare, as Hornby's big mistake.

"It was a great idea in principle but extremely dangerous in practice. Young kids would go to one of the Meccano dealers and buy this as a spare part. This was one of the great things about Meccano. You could buy spare parts; you didn't just have to stick with the sets. But if you bought the circular saw, you were buying something that was potentially dangerous. It could really inflict serious injury because you'd have it rotating with a motor at high speed, and there was no protection, and a naive young boy could put his finger on it and have it cut open. Hornby realized after a couple of years that this toy was dangerous and withdrew it from the market. As a result they are very rare, though there are a few around. I was fortunate in getting one and adding it to my collection about three years ago. It certainly was, in terms of a marketing concept, an error."

Ed Barclay stood up and stretched. Colin Hoare yawned. It was clearly time for me to go. But I had one more question. I fiddled with my drink and cleared my throat.

"I was wondering," I said, pointing towards the dining-room, "I was wondering what that is?"

Ed beamed and made a bee-line to the dining-room. Colin smiled ruefully. I was pointing at an enormous Meccano structure. Ed was already struggling with whatever it was and calling to Colin for help. The two of them humped it onto the dining-room table with considerable effort. It wasn't only big, it was also heavy. It looked like something Rube Goldberg's dim nephew might have assembled. Sitting on the table, it almost touched the ceiling. Up close it appeared to be a Meccano miniaturization of an amusement park. There was the roller coaster part and the Wild Mouse part, but it also had pulleys and elevators and a section that looked like the rollers at the supermarket where you put your box full of groceries. Ed was grinning like a big-game hunter.

"What," I asked, "does it do?"

"All it does is roll ping-pong balls round a massive configuration through different routes and spirals. It takes ten minutes for a ball to go round the whole machine. I call it Government Operations. The centre spiral is a four-foot-long Archimedean screw, which carries the balls right to the top. I call that part the inflationary spiral. As the balls roll down round and round and round, that's the spending power of the dollar. And so it goes on. There's the Cabinet Shuffle where the ball rolls backward and forward. It's the same old faces but different places. Right at the end of the machine is a little guy cranking a handle around, to make it look like he's driving the machine. I call him the taxpayer. It's a typical government machine because it expends a vast amount of energy and does nothing at all. All it really does is waste energy. Would you like to see it work?"

They started the machine up. It began sedately enough. The balls began an elegant climb up a sort of barber pole affair – the Ladder of Inflation. They began jostling down a set of stairs and through Foreign Policy, when all of a sudden something went wrong. There were ping-pong balls flying all over the room, and Colin and Ed, and Ed's wife, Holly, who came running from the kitchen, were scrambling around the dining-room picking up balls and stuffing them back into the machine. Ed was muttering something about the gears and his nephews. When things didn't seem to improve after several minutes, I quietly said my goodbyes. As I left, the machine was still whirring and clattering on the dining-room table, there were ping-pong balls flying around, and Ed and Colin and Holly were bouncing around after them.

"Just a moment," said Ed. "I'll see you to the door."

"It's OK," I said. "I'll let myself out." It was weird. But quite wonderful.

ONLY THE GREATEST GAME OF MONOPOLY EVER PLAYED

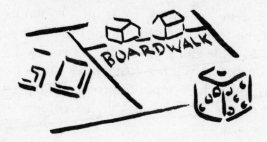

I am sitting at a table, and I am feeling anxious. The man sitting beside me is fiddling confidently with a pair of dice. I wish he would just throw them so that the game would begin. Once something starts I usually feel better. The man at my side, however, is in no hurry. He doesn't seem to sense my apprehension. I shift in my chair and my gaze wanders across the table to the man directly opposite me. He stares intently back. For an instant our eyes lock. When I look away, I can sense that he is still staring.

The man's name is David Brooks, and he is the reason I am here. I have been told that he is the Best Monopoly Player in Canada. David Brooks has represented Canada internationally in world-class Monopoly. He has not been beaten, at home, in championship play, for eight years.

When I was younger, I squandered endless rainy afternoons in summer cottages, hunched over stained Monopoly boards. My friends and I made Kraft pizza from the box, and we never finished a game without someone waving a fist full of cash and asking intently if we could *imagine* what it would be like to play with *real* money.

Well, David Brooks has played Monopoly on the Boardwalk in Atlantic City in a game where the winner walked away with $15,160, which happens to be all the money in the bank. That's $15,160 American dollars. That's *real* money.

And here he is, sitting in front of Illinois Avenue, staring at me from the other side of the board.

I asked for this game to be set up because I wanted to face the champ. I wanted to take my shot. I was given directions, over the telephone, to an industrial park on the edge of the city. I was told to come when it was dark.

I did not have any trouble finding the warehouse we are sitting in. It is on a road of warehouses in a neighbourhood of warehouses where nobody would bother driving at night. The only people I saw as I got close were a group of men warming themselves by a fire they had built in a forty-five gallon drum. I have seen men do this before, but that was in New York City, never on the edge of my town. I let myself into the warehouse and found the executive office in the north corner. I didn't expect it to be so posh. The champ and his two friends were sitting at a glistening oak table beneath a tapestry when I arrived. They had just polished off an Italian meal. The game was already set up – with an empty place at the board for me.

The champ, who is thirty-two, didn't say anything as I came in. He just nodded. His friend Joel stood up and stretched his arm out towards me. As we shook hands I noticed that he was wearing a diamond ring in the shape of a horseshoe. Very nice, I thought. A gambler. I looked at the third man, who turned to me and smiled.

"Look at Dave as the heavyweight champion of the world," he said. "Joel is his sparring partner. I'm here as the punching bag."

I like the analogy. This is a non-championship bout. It is the training camp in the Catskills. It is like I am stepping into the ring with Mohammed Ali. Maybe I will land a lucky punch.

Suddenly Diamond Ring clears his throat.

"Are we ready?" he asks.

David goes over the rules.

"We pay our fines to the bank, *not*," he says, looking at me, "into a FREE PARKING pile in the middle of the board."

FREE PARKING, he explained earlier, keeps weak players in the game long after they should be gone. FREE PARKING makes games drag on. A good Monopoly game lasts one-and-a-half to two hours.

"And," he repeats, apparently for my benefit, "no $400 for landing on GO."

Diamond Ring looks around the table one more time and finally hands the dice to me.

"Throw," he says with a smile.

I land on Baltic Avenue, the purple one. It costs $60. It is the cheapest property on the board. I look up. Everyone is looking at me. I curl my lips disdainfully.

"Pass," I say.

There is an auction for the property I have scornfully snubbed. I watch slack-jawed while everyone bids furiously. Diamond Ring gets it for $160. This shakes me up.

As we tumble around the board, they snap up every property in sight. I land on the B and O Railroad.

"Sold," I cry, catching on to the spirit of things. There is an awkward pause.

"Fool," says Diamond Ring.

They don't like the Railroads. You can't build on them.

There is another auction for another property. I am

bidding. The Champ is the auctioneer.

"Going once, going twice, ssss. . . "

A millisecond after he begins to say, "sold," I interrupt to raise the bid.

"Two hundred," I cry.

". . . sssold." He finishes the word looking at me. "You were too late."

Everyone nods. These guys don't fool around. Especially the Champ.

> "That's how we play Monopoly when we get together. We play to win, and we don't let anybody get anything for nothing. If you make late bids you don't get the property. We play cutthroat. That's the way we like to play; the way we all like to play. I don't let anybody get anything for nothing, and when I want something I ask quite a bit for it."

I am beginning to feel a little bit like the country rube who has wandered into a clip joint with the family inheritance. The worst is yet to come. I stumble around the board a few more times until there are no more properties left to buy.

It is time to start dealing, and I am not prepared for what happens. It is like sitting at a dinner table with a family full of auctioneers, each one trying to out-hustle the other. The speed of the chatter is mesmerizing. The complexity of the frantically proposed deals almost incomprehensible. These aren't the friendly trades I am used to ("Hey, Uncle David, how about I give you Oriental for North Carolina?"). These are three and four-layer swaps that are complex enough to give Henry Kissinger pause. For speed, the men at the table are referring to properties by their colours rather than the names printed on the board.

"You make the deal with him. He gets the Purples, you get the Blues. You'll give me the Oranges for the Park Place. You're willing to take the lesser of these two properties knowing that I'm the one that's going to have to deal with you because I sit out the game and get zilch. If he's willing to do it I can't stop him, but I don't see any reason why you don't want the Yellows since you're cash rich ... roll ... Waterworks. If we'd had that we would be rich."

As the proposed deals rebound around the room, I sit dumbly in front of my cards, nodding and thinking that this doesn't sound like any game I have ever played. Though I am feeling completely intimidated, I know that I too have to do a deal. The alternative is to go without a monopoly and look foolish. The Champ and Diamond Ring are busy structuring something on the other side of the table which is beyond my comprehension, so when Punching Bag turns to me and suggests a straight swap – Vermont for St. Charles or, as he says, Blue for Purple – I am ready to deal.

There is suddenly dead silence at the table. The Champ has fixed me in a hypnotic stare.

"Don't do it," he says menacingly.

He launches into a feverish sermon explaining why the trade would be the stupidest thing I could do to myself, to him, and to the game in general. Diamond Ring is staring at me like a Mafia hit man. I am having an out-of-body experience.

Not sure why I am doing it, I consummate the trade. The Champ shakes his head sadly.

Later in the night the Champ will tell me that it really wasn't a bad deal after all. He tells me that he always intervenes in trades and tries his best to run them off the rails. He does this to prevent anyone else from getting a monopoly. He says he has a number of strategies he employs to intimidate people.

"You can look at a deal and analyse it to the point where you can see that someone is getting the worst end of it. If you are good enough to pick up on it, you take their side and emphasize to them that the other guy is getting a better deal, that he's got more money, that he's able to build quicker, look where you are on the board. There's a lot of things involved. Take his side and tell him he's getting a bad deal. Maybe he's not, but you are conning him. You'll get him not to deal. What do I get out of that? I just prolong the game until my position is somehow stronger. And maybe I can get in on the deals where it won't hurt me as bad. Whereas most people, if the deal doesn't involve them, they'll just remain quiet."

I always thought Monopoly was a game of pure luck. The Champ disagrees.

"Two-thirds luck," he says. "One-third skill."

The game opens and closes with luck, but the luck is subordinate to skill at the mid-point of the match. Luck may determine which properties you land on, and consequently buy at the opening of the game, but it's the player's skill that allows him to structure deals that will enhance his position. Finally, once the monopolies are put in place, luck returns to determine who lands where.

Two-thirds luck, perhaps, but the men I am facing play all the angles. Every time someone rolls the dice, the Champ picks them up and holds them until the next player is ready to go. He does this, he tells me, so he can control the game. This way nothing can happen without him knowing.

They all have their theories.

"Don't buy the Railroads," says Diamond Ring, "because you can't improve the Railroads."

The same goes for the Utilities. And stay away from the Greens (Pennsylvania, North Carolina and Pacific). They are nice, but they are too expensive to develop. Of course, as if you didn't already know, grab Park Place and Boardwalk if you can get them.

Punching Bag is particularly concerned with the dice.

"Because the game is played with dice, it is certainly a help to know what the probability is of certain numbers on the dice coming up. The number seven, has more probability than any other number on the dice. There are more combinations on the dice that add up to seven than any other number. So if you had someone who was approaching your properties, and you wanted to build on them, you would count the number of spaces that that man would have to move his piece to get there. And if it did come to a seven, then that would be the property you would put most of your houses on, because the whole game revolves around the probability of a person landing on a property that has been capitalized or built on. You've got to use every trick in your favour, so you play the odds of the dice."

The dice rolled my way most of the night. I landed my lucky punch at 10:15. I blindsided Diamond Ring, Punching Bag and the Champ. I won. I did it with the hotels I had put up on Virginia, States Avenue and St. Charles Place. The Purple ones, the ones the Champ didn't want me to deal for. I'd made a lucky deal, but I felt like a million dollars. The Champ seemed unperturbed. He stood up and stretched and said he had to go bowling. As he prepared to leave, I asked him if he planned to play in the next Canadian championship. He said he would be there. I wondered if he had ever thought of retiring undefeated.

> "I could retire three-time undefeated champion. I'm the only one ever to win the title three times. There are two other people who have their names on the trophy twice, but nobody has it three times – just me. I might retire, but I doubt it. There's a lot at stake, but I think I'll be there."

The elusive lure of one more big score has kept many champions in many games long after they should have retired. But there is no denying that $15,000 is a lot of money. Especially for a game of Monopoly.

Maybe, I thought, as I climbed into my car and drove out of the industrial park, maybe I should be there, too. The kid from the CBC. The Monopoly Champion of Canada. The shooter. The big-shot real estate dealer. Images of big red hotels and little green houses spun through my head as I wound my way back to the highway.

I had forgotten about the guys at the oil barrel. They were still huddled around their fire as I drove by. They didn't look like they had moved since the game began.

The hot-shot developer stopped his car. I wanted to know what was happening. It was, they explained to me, a picket line. They were on strike. I stayed and talked to them for a while and warmed my hands by their fire. What, I asked, would they do with more money if they won their strike. I was feeling flush, my head still full of hotels and handfuls of cash. Caesar, a man from Jamaica, answered right away.

"I'd buy a house, man," he said, looking at me.

A house. Of course.

SOMETHING ABOUT
BURIED TREASURE

You know, of course, who the metal detector people are. They are the guys who appear to be vacuuming the sand at the beach. They move along the edge of the water waving a stick that looks like a golf club with a Frisbee stuck on the end. They also wear earphones, which beep every time the Frisbee part passes over buried metal. What they are looking for is money and lost jewellery. What they get is a lot of nails, bottle caps and tabs from aluminium cans. But they also get money and jewellery, and I have always wanted to know how much. Which is why I decided to go to the regular monthly meeting of the Canadian Discovery Association.

There were probably fifty members in the club room when I arrived. All very tanned. All men, and all getting on towards retirement. Well, they weren't *all* men. There were four women hovering around the edge of the room, but they were clearly members' wives, not full-fledged members in their own right. As I walked into the room I sensed a festive mood. If I hadn't already known what was going on, I might have guessed that these were renegade members of the Thunder Bay Canadian Legion. Maybe they had dipped into the till and taken a two-week break in Costa Rica and had got together to cook up a story that might explain where the missing money was and where they had got all the sun. Except it really was the regular monthly meeting of the Canadian Discovery Association.

There is a coffee break and I introduce myself to two men who are standing apart from everyone else and talking with great animation. I am a journalist and wonder if they would care to talk to me for awhile about their hobby.

They both looked surprised and stared at me as if I have made some serious social blunder. Not here they say. Meet us outside. Later.

It was dark outside. We were sitting under the stars on a small knoll behind the meeting hall. We could have been in the country somewhere. The campfire could have just flickered out. Gus and Bob introduced themselves. They are, they say, best friends. They are both retired, both ex-POWs. Bob was captured at Dieppe. Gus was shot down over Holland. They met three years ago through their mutual love of metal detecting.

As I pulled out my tape recorder, Gus demurred. Bob had written a book, he said. He should do all the talking. Bob cleared his throat and proceeded to tell me about one of Gus's perfect finds.

"It happened at an old abandoned schoolhouse from the 1800s. There was a little slope out front, a very slight incline, and Gus figured that may be where the kids would sit on the grass. He started up and got a signal right away. When he was done he had got about five or six dimes, a couple of nickels and maybe thirteen pennies. And there was a few threads of cloth to show him that there had been a little purse. Maybe some mother had given it to the kid and said, 'after school go to the grocery store and get so and so, and don't lose the purse,' and the kid had sat there and lost the purse. So that may have been, say, seventy-five years ago. And in your imagination it's a great thrill because you think, geez, try to picture back, what type of kid was this. Maybe she had a little bonnet or a long dress. Or maybe it was a little boy wearing knickers or something. Your imagination comes alive."

Gus nodded in the darkness and told me that there are two fundamental schools of metal detecting – the water school and the land school.

The land people, he said, look for lost money. The fun comes from finding old coins. The older the coin, the bigger the kick. Gus and Bob know people who have found coins that date back before Canada was issuing currency – coins issued when individual merchants struck their own money.

They explained how some guys work old farms, hoping to find buried and forgotten caches. There are stories, they said, of $5,000 and $10,000 bonanzas. Guys who know what they are doing will figure out where the farm kitchen was and search all the ground that would have been in sight of the kitchen window. A good place to look is under old fence posts.

When Bob and Gus work the land they usually work city parks. Parks can be rich hunting grounds. Sometimes they'll get old city maps and look for parks that no longer exist – parks that have become schoolyards or parking lots. Bob has a favourite trick he uses when he covers abandoned parkland.

"I always look for oak trees, for the simple reason that people have a habit of sitting under an oak tree with their back to it. Some of the expert detectors come around and see a big old tree, and they'll mark off maybe a ten-foot square with cord. And then they'll go over this square, back and forth, back and forth, and pull out every piece of junk, take out every bottle cap, every pull tab, every nail, every bobby pin, whatever. Clean the ground of surface junk. They'll spend a day at that sometimes, even in a ten-foot square. And they'll come back the next day and get the deep coins. Because your surface junk interferes with your good coins. They are usually hidden deep."

Gus and Bob spend most of their time in the water. They go out in chest waders two or three times a week, and pull their metal detectors behind them on inner tubes. They start in April when there is still ice on a lake and keep going until the ice comes back in the fall. Bob says Gus can stay in the water for eight hours straight without taking a break. They like beaches the best, because people's bodies shrink in cold water and rings have a tendency to fall off. You see, when Gus and Bob do land, they are looking for coins. In the water they are looking for jewellery.

"You get a kick when you get a coin or silver ring, but the big thrill is when you bring up your scoop and you see gold. It's that age-old feeling like the prospectors had of finding *gold*. It's a sort of romantic thing, you know. Even though we're modern, you still have that same feeling. You get a bang out of it when you see gold in the scoop. It's like, 'I've got GOLD,' you know. It's the colour of gold that excites you."

I was mesmerized by these two men. We sat on the grass in the darkness and talked about gold jewellery and buried coins for hours. We also talked about the war. Bob had escaped from his POW camp twice. Once he was loose inside Germany for over a month before he was re-captured. Bob and Gus have nicknames for each other, and they keep score of the gold items they each find. They tabulate the score once a year. Bob made it clear that Gus is always the winner.

"I call him Goldfinger. Last year he beat me out by about three to one. This year it was about seven to one. One day I almost caught up to him. It was a Saturday. I got five in one day. But I can't say where because we don't divulge our secrets to anybody. We have maybe sixty or seventy-five people in our club and they watch you like a hawk. They try to find out where you go. You sort of have to watch that you're not followed, because everybody wants to find the good place. Gus and I go together, and we're the only two that know where we go. Other members will ask how you did during the week. 'Well, I got two rings, three rings, or I didn't get any,' or whatever. Soon as they see you've got a ring, someone asks, 'Oh, where did you get it?' 'In the water.' Some are nervy enough to say, 'Where?' but I'm sorry, we don't say that. Because if you ask them where they found a certain thing they won't tell you."

Somewhere near midnight I asked Bob if you could get rich with a metal detector.

"You never get rich, no. In Gus's and my case we don't do it for the money. We're in it for the thrill of finding things. We're both hoarders, we both collect. We never sell a thing. We may give some away to

family. In my case I just shove 'em in an old album.
Gus shoves his in his jewellery cases. We look at them
and we gloat over them. We love them, you know.
And each thing you look at you remember where you
were when you found it. So we have something in
common, and we enjoy our hobby."

"I'm seventy-four, you know, but I don't feel my
age. I figure as long as you've got something active to
do, like a good hobby, you're OK. In the spring,
summer and fall I'm alive because of this hobby. In
the winter I die."

Gus began to fidget. They were planning to go out early
the next morning and he said he wanted to get some
sleep. I walked with them to Gus's car and noticed the big
government map that was sharing the back seat with a
wool sweater and a pair of wool socks. It was the kind of
map that you use when you go into the bush. As they
pulled out of the parking lot they honked the horn softly
and waved. They were both retired. Worried not about
growing old, but about being followed. Looking for
secret places, hunting for buried treasure, revelling in
each other's company.

A SHORT HISTORY OF THE YO-YO

I bought my first YO-YO return top in 1956. It was purple and had diamond studs set into the wood on each side. The diamonds were actually pieces of cut glass, but they looked terrific, and it never dawned on any of us that they weren't precious stones. The Cheerio Toys and Games Company abetted this deception by calling my model "The Jewelled Satellite". My Jewelled Satellite cost me ninety-eight cents. This was back in the days before shrink-wrap, so when I went down to Westminster Avenue to buy my YO-YO, I was able to pick it right out of the cardboard display box that lay on the counter at the Library Gift Shop. I held it carefully in my palm and judiciously compared its weight to a pale-blue one, holding them both out in front of me before deciding that the purple Jewelled Satellite had been made for me. I paid for it out of my allowance.

Like most kids who grew up in the fifties, I learned how to use my YO-YO in the park beside my school. The instructors appeared unannounced one autumn afternoon and set up shop like a travelling medicine show.

They wore blue windbreakers with a big YO-YO crest on the back, over a white shirt and tie, and showed up in the park every afternoon for a week. Then they disappeared as mysteriously as they had come.

Each afternoon they lined us up by the Carolina poplars and taught us tricks. One by one we had to step forward and try each trick for them. If we got it wrong they didn't give us what today we politely call 'feedback'. They *criticized* us.

I remember the whirring sound the YO-YOs made as they spun up and down. A line of YO-YOs whirring in the afternoon sun sounds like a field of wheat being harvested. You'd throw your YO-YO away and it would lie there "sleeping" at the end of the string, waiting for you to flick your finger the way the Queen might flick her finger to summon a corgi. If you got it right, you'd flick and your YO-YO would snap back, right away, faster than you'd think possible.

I was sitting in Al Gallo's living-room hunched over an old scrapbook, flipping through his YO-YO clippings. Al Gallo was sitting in his favourite armchair smiling at me. No single individual had more to do with my YO-YO lessons than Al Gallo. For forty years Al Gallo was Mr YO-YO, not only in Canada, but in the world.

YO-YOs began in Canada, he said, in the 1920s, with a guy by the name of Sam Dubiner. Dubiner owned a plastics company, a few other business concerns and, on the side, the Canadian rights to two toys known as the Bo-Lo Bat and the YO-YO. One day Sam had this idea that he could promote the YO-YO by sending demonstrators across the country. It turned out to be one of the most brilliant toy promotions ever dreamed up anywhere. Period.

Sam hired about a dozen university students, called them instructors and set about introducing them to his toy. The classes, held in the back of one of his warehouses, often lasted more than ten hours, and by the end of each day more than one instructor left with his YO-YO finger bleeding from the constant thumping of the wooden disc. When he was satisfied they knew enough, Dubiner sent his boys across the country. When they arrived in a town, they moved from park to park, showing kids tricks and handing out prizes. The idea was that the kids who took the free lessons would go into the school yards and teach everyone else about the toy. The idea worked perfectly. The YO-YO is probably the only toy in history that came with its own instructor. Whenever they left a town, the only thing the instructors left behind was a YO-YO craze.

Dubiner created the first Canadian YO-YO craze in 1929. Ten years later he decided the time was ripe for another kick at the cat. That's when Al Gallo came aboard. Al was one of fifteen young men Dubiner hired to help create the second great wave. Al Gallo remembers that basic training had an almost military flavour to it.

"We had to wear our hair a certain way, and we had to dress a certain way, always with a shirt and tie on, because the most important thing in his books was the fact that we were teaching children. We were in contact with children right across Canada. We had to have good teeth, we had to have clean fingernails, and we had to be well groomed, shoes shined at all times. His philosophy was just because a child buys a YO-YO, it doesn't mean we're through with them. His theory was if you teach the children how to use the item, they will keep playing, and if they keep playing they're going to break strings. We sold an awful lot of strings. We might have been in the YO-YO business, but I guess any child that bought a YO-YO spent more money on the strings than he did on the YO-YO."

Al Gallo was twenty years old when he signed on as a YO-YO instructor. His parents wanted him to go to college, but Dubiner offered him thirteen dollars a week and the chance to travel across the country with his YO-YO. He went from Newfoundland to Victoria. Every week he carefully counted out two dollars to pay the boarding house where he had slept. He had to pay an extra thirty-five cents each night for dinner.

Al was so good at his job as a demonstrator that he soon found himself in charge of the day-to-day operation of the Cheerio Toys and Games Company. He slipped into the world of YO-YO as if he was born for that and nothing else. Around the World, Walk the Dog, Rock the Baby in the Cradle were the staple tricks of the trade. To these Gallo added tricks of his own – the Atomic Bomb, the Brain Twister, Double or Nothing, and something called the Skyrocket, where he took a sleeping YO-YO off his finger, threw it forty feet in the air and caught it in his pocket. There was instruction in the parks, complete with tests and badges. There was also the Odeon Theatre Saturday Morning Club ("Bring your YO-YO," said the signs), where a kid with a fast hand could win sweaters, jackets, bikes, radios and trophies. There was nothing like it anywhere else in the world. It was a uniquely Canadian phenomenon. Under Gallo and Dubiner, not only did the YO-YO's repertoire grow – so did its history. It wasn't just a toy. It was a weapon from the Philippines.

"The way I heard the story was that the natives carved this item out of wood or stone, maybe eighteen or twenty inches in diameter, and they would attach animal hide or vine to it and wind it up, and get up in the trees and shoot it down at small game or at one of their enemies. This is the story I heard. I also understand the name YO-YO means 'come back'. I don't know how true that is."

True or not, it was a great story. On an early promotion
tour, Dubiner hired Philippino men as demonstrators.
They wore black silk pyjamas with red sashes and per-
formed their routines while standing on the counters of
Woolworth and Kresge stores across the country.

Somewhere along the line Sam Dubiner sent Al Gallo
to the United States. When Al got there he found that
someone else already owned the rights to the name
YO-YO. But that didn't stop him. He simply changed the
name of his product. He called it the Cheerio Return Top
and blew the American competition out of the water.
When he came back to Canada he bought the Cheerio
Toys and Games Company from Dubiner and ran it with
his wife for thirty-five years. They never had any children
of their own. Instead they spent almost thirty-five years
on the road with every other kid in the country.

In 1978, when Al Gallo retired, he sold the Cheerio
Toys and Games Company to Parker Brothers. And in
1981 Parker Brothers stopped all the promotions. They
declared there would be no more travelling instructors
and no more contests in the parks. They couldn't compete with video games, they said. Nor could they afford to
pay demonstrators modern wages. They say they still sell
100,000 YO-YOs a year, but they concede business will
never be like it was in the glory days.

Al Gallo says that's too bad. He says when he toured the
country with his instructors, no country in the world (not
even the Philippines) turned out YO-YO players that
could compete with Canadian kids.

"Canadian kids in the past have been the best YO-YO
players in the world. Much better than the American
kids, because the American kids, they bought YO-
YOs – there's millions of dollars' worth of YO-YOs
sold in the States every year – but the kids don't know
how to do the tricks. The Canadian kids can outplay

anybody in the world. If they ever had an Olympic
tournament in YO-YOs, the Canadian kids would win
first, second and third prizes. In my lifetime I made
Canadians the world's best YO-YO players, and that
makes me feel good. I loved it, too, you know?
Especially when I was demonstrating. I loved it.
Simply because the kids figured you were a hero. The
kids used to follow you around and say, hey, champ,
do this and do that. That was my only claim to
fame – playing with the YO-YO. They used to call me
King of the YO-YOs. That's what they called me."

Al Gallo made more than a million dollars teaching
Canadian kids the finer points of the YO-YO. Today he
lives part-time in Florida and part-time in Toronto. When
he isn't playing golf he paints oil reproductions of works
by the great masters. Sometimes his friends ask him to
bring his YO-YOs to their grandchildren's birthday parties. He says he likes to do that.

As I was preparing to leave, Al asked me if I would like
to see some stuff. He scurried into his bedroom and came
back with a YO-YO in each hand. He was swinging them
around his head the way I imagine Wild Bill Hickok would
have swung his guns. Then he stopped in the middle of
the room, smiled and "walked the dog" with both YO-
YOs at once.

"Nice," I said. "How long can you make them sleep
for?"

"Oh, I've made a YO-YO sleep for about a minute. A
minute is pretty long. Down in the States the kids call
it sticking. We didn't know what they were talking
about when they said, 'Make it stick', but it turned
out they meant the sleeper – making the YO-YO sleep
down at the bottom. Then you jerk your finger and it
comes up. Watch out, here's Spank the Baby and

Poke Him in the Tummy. Do you want to see the
Man on the Flying Trapeze?"

"You made a million bucks doing this," I said.

"Oh, yeah," he laughed. "A little over." Al Gallo
was beaming. "There's the Man on the Flying Trapeze. You put him on, you throw him around."

There is a funny little move that many great athletes
share. It's a special little kick of the leg. Golfers do it when
they sink a long putt. Bowlers do it when they get a strike.
One leg kicks out joyfully and punches the air. Every time
Al Gallo did a trick, his left leg shot out like an exclama-
tion mark. At sixty-nine years old, and after fifty years of
YO-YOing, he still couldn't contain his joy at going
Round the World. He was standing in the middle of his
living-room, smiling like a ten-year-old kid. His eyes
sparkled as his YO-YOs criss-crossed in mid-air.

"You look like the cat that swallowed the mouse," I
said, smiling.

Gallo kept flipping his YO-YO. He was grinning from
ear to ear.

"Here's one called the machine gun," he said, laughing.

THE SNEAKY ART OF A BASEBALL GROUNDSKEEPER

I don't like domed stadiums. I hate going indoors to watch an outdoor game. Simply put, I am opposed to things that come between me and the sun. Philosophically, I am appalled by what domes tell us about our relationship to the natural world. It's as if we couldn't bear the sight of real dirt. As if rain was offensive. As if no one should ever feel cold. Hello plastic grass. Hello engineers. Goodbye loam and fertilizer. Goodbye to peat moss soaking up puddles in centre field. Goodbye groundskeepers, good men of the soil.

Groundskeepers.

I am, you see, a baseball fan.

And as I, and many like me, mourn the passing of grass stains, rain delays, make-up games, outfield slides, long grass, high grass, sweet grass . . . dirt, damn it – as we see these things slip sadly away, we should not forget to nod goodbye to the groundskeeper, too. There will come a day, too soon I fear, when there will be no groundskeepers left in the major leagues.

Too bad.

It has been said that playing baseball against a team with a good groundskeeper is like facing a team with an extra man in the field. This is a hard truth to swallow for those of us who follow baseball in Canada. Not only must we suffer the indignity of ball parks better suited to demolition derbies than double plays, we must also accept the fact that while some teams can turn for help to men of the soil, all Canadians can do is turn to rug cleaners. Groundskeepers and their sneaky bag of tricks have no home in Canada.

Roger Bossard is the groundskeeper for the Chicago White Sox. He believes that the difference between victory or defeat can turn on a blade of grass. He is a man who gardens with intensity.

> "I have a four-blend grass on my infield. The reason for that – and this is gospel, I'm a devout Catholic – is that there are some days when I will want to cut the grass short. Say we are going against a team that doesn't have a lot of offense, and our offensive capabilities are greater than theirs. If I cut the grass short, the ball is going to scoot through the infield faster, which will help us, on balance, more than it will help them. But when you cut the grass short during hot weather, you become very susceptible to disease. By having a mixture of four blends, the disease will maybe only attack two of the blends. So if I do get a disease, my infield will still be green. Four blends give me the elbow room to do more."

Bossard says that during the 1983 season, depending on who his team was facing, he would vary the length of the infield grass in Comiskey Park anywhere from one inch short to two and a half inches long. He says that between short and long he chose about twelve different grass lengths. All of his gardening decisions were made to give his team, the Chicago White Sox, an advantage. If, for instance, Chicago was facing a team that was stronger offensively, a team that hit more than Chicago, then he would let the infield grass grow long. All the hits that bounced in the infield that day would be slowed by the long grass. Because the opposition would probably be hitting more than the home team, more of the opposition hits would be slowed, and that would be to Chicago's advantage.

Bossard says that before he uses any of his gardening tricks, he takes a careful look at the record of both teams about to play. Once he is loaded with statistics, he can, he says, do all sorts of things. Take water, for instance. Bossard loves water. He knows, from studying the books, that when his team faces a low-ball pitcher, about 53 percent of Chicago's hits will bounce within an eight-foot radius of home plate. So every time a low-ball pitcher comes to town, Bossard makes sure the ground in front of home plate is hard and dry, so that those Chicago hits get a good bounce. On the other hand, if it happens to be the Chicago pitcher who specializes in the low ball, Bossard will go out before the game with a garden hose and water the living daylights out of that eight-foot circle, so that every time the opposition hits a grounder, it will bounce in the muck and be slowed down for the Chicago fielders.

Bossard's greatest moment with water came the afternoon Chicago was scheduled to play a team renowned for base stealing.

"These guys could run real good. The main forte of that team was running. Our orders were to make sure nobody stole second base. What Dad and myself did was we wet down the line going from first to second for about twenty feet. That meant that if any runner were to try to steal, he's not going to get real good footing. The key to this trick is to do it so the opposition doesn't know. To do that, the night before, we opened up the soil with a shovel and put a lot of moisture going down five or six inches so the ground was real soft underneath. Then we put a little sand on the top so it looks dry. We're starting the game, Bill North is the lead-off man, and there are forty-thousand people in the stands. North walks on four pitches. He goes to first base. Dad and myself of course know what we've done, and that Bill North is probably going to try and steal. Well, he did. Except he took about two and a half steps and fell right on his face. The catcher threw the ball to first base and tagged him out. Well, I got to tell you, the crowd went crazy. Needless to say, Dad and I felt exuberant."

Another area that a creative groundskeeper can work with is the pitcher's mound. According to the rule book, the pitcher's mound should be ten inches above home plate. Every inch higher is an advantage for the pitcher. That advantage is magnified if the pitcher happens to rely on the fastball because, by raising the pitcher, you add speed to his pitches.

It is part of the umpires' job to keep a wary eye on the height of the mound. They measure mounds by nailing a string into the ground just behind the pitcher's rubber. Then they run the string in a straight line until it touches home plate. At home, they take a line level and make sure the string is sitting straight, then they measure the distance from the string to the ground.

The next man I spoke to, who is also a major league groundskeeper, asked to remain anonymous. He, too, is an intense gardener. And he, too, has developed his own bag of tricks. Because his team has an abundance of fast-ball pitchers, he specializes in raising the pitcher's mound.

"There are lots of ways of cheating. The simplest is to build up your mound in excess of ten inches – let's just use twelve inches as an example. Now, once you've built it you've got to measure it. So when the umpire asks for a ten-inch stick at home plate, you give him a twelve-inch stick, though you only mark it as being ten inches. If the umpires don't measure the height of the stick, well, that's one way of doing it. Another way of doing it is to build your mound up to a twelve-inch height, but then build the home plate up two inches. By that I mean the whole area, not just the home plate itself. You build up the area near home plate and crown it out to the home plate circle. So home plate is crowned two inches, but the difference to where the batters feet are, is minimal. The pitching mound is still up two inches above the legal limit, and that benefits a power pitcher."

Finally, a groundskeeper can play with the foul lines. Everybody knows that the Blue Jays don't bunt. Their manager doesn't like the bunt. So when the Blue Jays come into an opponent's park, chances are if anyone bunts it will be the home team. Someone who understands the inner game of groundskeeping can work with information like that. Roger Bossard says it is common practice for groundskeepers to tilt the foul lines one way or the other to help their team. If their team likes to bunt, they'll tilt the lines "fair", so bunted balls rolling along the line are more likely to roll into play. If their team doesn't use the bunt, they'll do the opposite and tilt the lines "foul". Roger Bossard says he does it all the time in Chicago.

"The key to doing these tricks is getting away with it. Any Joe Blow can go out and say, I'm going to raise the foul line by four inches. But what good is that if the opposing team comes out and spots it? Now the key is to tilt it just enough so you know it, and the ball players that you tell on your side know it, yet the opposing team can't see it. I'll tell you how to do it. Picture a field. Now imagine the third-base line, which goes down third base all the way to the outfield. Now on a natural turf field, that line is put down on dirt – there is dirt on each side of the white line. So I actually have three feet of dirt that I can manicure to a certain grade to keep that ball fair. The opposing team can't actually see it, because of the width of dirt I have to work with. But if you have less dirt – like there are some grounds that have the grass coming right up to the foul line – needless to say, you can't tilt your lines."

Is all this unfair?

Well, maybe. Or maybe not.

But I think it is a lot more real than playing baseball on plastic grass in stadiums with giant-sized cartoon characters bounding up and down the aisles.

The arguments advanced by pea-brained politicians in favour of domes have never impressed me. In Toronto they said a dome would attract tourists. I don't believe it. Do you know anyone who has gone to Dallas to see the dome? On the other hand, I dream of going to Chicago to visit Wrigley Field. Or New York to see Yankee Stadium. Or Detroit. Oh Detroit. And I know I'm not alone. If someone really wanted to attract tourists to their town, they would build a tiny perfect ball park. It would be almost round and made of brick, and have lots of arches and ivy. An intimate ball park with a sense of what's important. A park that would use real tickets printed on a printing press instead of spat out of a computer. One that would welcome the wind and the sun, the mud and the rain and, above all else, real grass. I, for one, would travel a long way to see baseball played on real grass, in a park where somewhere, in a corridor lost under the stands, is a wooden door with a frosted glass window. Painted in gold letters on the window is one word: Groundskeeper.

OF BOYS, BALLS AND BRICK WALLS

On a recent spring morning, finding myself awake earlier than usual, I got up, fixed some coffee and, with nothing better to do, snuck out the back door. Alone in the backyard, I decided to do something I hadn't done for thirty years. I set off for the elementary school yard in my new neighbourhood. I wanted to witness the early-morning rituals of arrival.

For the first time in my life I was the first person there. Sipping my coffee, I sank down behind the chain-link fence in a corner of the yard beside a tree, and I waited. The first boy came just after seven. He was carrying a tennis ball, and as it popped on the pavement, memories from a milder time bounced into my mind.

That night at dinner, it was suddenly very important to instruct my family on *how things used to be.* I wanted to tell them everything about the comings and goings in the boys' yard at Elizabeth Ballantyne School circa 1950. Things that happened before the second bell.

It was the teenager at the table who brought home to me just how arcane my childhood has become.

"Marbles and chestnuts? What's the point of marbles and chestnuts? I have never seen a bunch of kids playing marbles and chestnuts. Marbles are just something that your old aunts or grandmothers give you and end up in the bottom of your drawer. I've never played with marbles. I used to throw them at people, but I never played with them. Chestnuts I have never even heard of. I think that's just a game made up by authors of children's books. What's the point of banging a couple of chestnuts together?"

After dinner I slouched to the telephone. I phoned old friends. I wanted to compare their memories with mine. And, yes, there were marbles. In Montreal West there was a strip of grass that separated the sidewalk from the road. It was about three feet wide – a sort of common ground whose purpose I never really fathomed. Maybe it actually was put there, as I used to believe, for playing marbles. It was supposed to be grass. But over the years, on our way to and from school, we wore the grass away. Me and kids like Ron Doleman.

"It was just dirt with two or three marble holes in each block. And so it could take you instead of five minutes to go from Brock to E.B. [Brock was the street I lived on, Elizabeth Ballantyne School was known as E.B.] . . . it could take you an hour. So you would set out at seven-thirty in the morning, if it was a good marble day, and people would be waiting at the marble holes. The pots were different sizes. Some were square, some were shallow. And you would try to go to the spot that you wanted to play on."

The school yard, when you got to it, was segregated. We, the boys, went to our side, and the girls went to the other. I have no idea what went on in the girls' yard.

Sometimes baseball, I think. Mostly skipping. Hopscotch. And a game they played with their feet and a large elastic band.

The boys' yard was an alley that ran along the south side of the school, and the first thing you noticed about it were the lacrosse balls. There were lacrosse balls everywhere. No one played lacrosse. No one was even certain what lacrosse was. There were just hundreds of white India-rubber Viceroy lacrosse balls because lacrosse balls were the best balls to bounce off brick walls.

"We used to play a game called Ledgers. The brick wall went up about four feet and then there was this cement line that went in about two inches that was a perfect ledge. Now if you threw a lacrosse ball at the ledge, the ball bounced off the top of it so that it would pop back up, way up in the air, and that was called a Ledger. If you caught it – the Ledger – you got a point. If your throw went below the ledge, you were out and the other person would start throwing Ledgers. Now, Mr Tims noticed that the bricks were getting loose because lacrosse balls are very very hard, so we had to switch to tennis balls. But we would show up for the real challenges on the weekends when no one was around, and we'd use lacrosse balls."

When the lacrosse ball disappeared from the weekday scene, a new game arrived along with the tennis ball – "Stand-O", or maybe "Stand-All". The exact pronunciation of the game was one of the many mysteries of my youth. It was an embarrassing uncertainty I preferred to live with rather than ask about. It was a word that I learned to slur assertively. I didn't worry, except privately, about the meaning or the etymology. Like Ledgers, to play Stand-O you needed boys, balls and brick walls. Unlike Ledgers, you couldn't win a game of Stand-O, you could only lose it. Every time you did something wrong during the game, you were awarded what we used to call a baby. The first boy to accumulate five or maybe ten babies was the loser. Losers had to run the gauntlet, a jolly affair we picked up from the Iroquois Indians. The gauntlet consisted of two parallel lines of boys, facing each other. As you ran the gauntlet, your friends hit you – hopefully your bottom, fearfully your head or kidneys. If you didn't run the gauntlet, you were made to stand spread-eagled against the school wall, like you might for a police search. Then your classmates had the right to hurl the tennis ball at you from an agreed upon distance. They aimed for your ears or the back of your neck.

There were, thankfully, more cerebral pastimes. There was, as Dane Lanken reminded me, Stems.

"I don't know if Stems was played anywhere else other than Elizabeth Ballantyne School. There was a row of Carolina poplar trees at the side of the school. Poplars have big leaves with big strong thick stems, and it was these stems that the game was played with. Carolina poplars are the top of the line in the Stems game. Two kids would pick up stems and you would interlock them and pull one stem against the other and the stem that broke the other was the winner and became one year old. Once in a while you would find a stem that was practically unbreakable."

The object of Stems was to run a string of victories in a row and age your stem as much as possible. If someone managed to snap your stem, then their stem assumed all the years that had already accrued to yours. The temptation to lie about the age of your stem was too much for most of us, and the morality of the school yard accepted that and even more sophisticated manipulations. Teams of young swindlers would collude together to propel one stem towards old age and fame by matching it again and again against lesser stuff. That was OK. What was not tolerated was heavy-handedness. Any kind of outright cheating was outlawed. You would not, for instance, be allowed to string a length of piano wire through a stem to make it invincible.

Stems was an autumn game. So was chestnuts, also known as Conkers or Knockers. To play you would get a chestnut, drill a hole through it and thread a string through the hole. Then, taking turns, you would hold your chestnut by the string while other kids whacked it with nuts of their own. The object, like Stems, was to destroy your opponent's chestnut. Hours were spent curing chestnuts in the oven or, mysteriously, soaking them in vinegar. These two processes allegedly made the sensuous brown nuts indestructible. I never understood whether you were supposed to put the hole into the nut before or after you cured it. But that was of little importance, because the romance and adventure didn't come in the curing. The real romance, as Dane Lanken remembers, was in the search.

"I don't remember where the chestnuts came from. I certainly don't remember any chestnut trees in Montreal West. Somehow they just turned up. I do remember that late one summer my family went for a drive to Niagara Falls, and my brother and I were looking around the park there and we came across a chestnut tree that just at that time was dropping its chestnuts. The ground was littered with chestnuts in those prickly green things that they come in, and to my brother and me it was the El Dorado, the Bonanza. So we loaded up paper bags and boxes of these chestnuts and put them in my father's car and took them back with us to Montreal West. As it happened, that fall, chestnuts seemed to have passed.

It was no longer played in the school yard. And instead of having this gold mine all we had were bags of chestnuts that sat in my dad's garage for years afterwards before they finally hit the compost pile. When I grew up I planted a chestnut tree in my backyard with the game of chestnuts in mind. It hasn't produced chestnuts yet, but I have great expectations."

The boys' yard at E.B. lives in my mind as a Moroccan bazaar. Clusters of young boys quibbling and quarrelling. A place full of danger. Every morning when you came to school you came to risk the lives of your stems, or the existence of your chestnuts. You could watch some kid lose a month's worth of hockey cards in a game of shot kissers, leaners or just straight flip cards. You could risk your wrist in Scissors/Paper/Stone. Every time your opponent covered your rock with his paper he would lick his first and second fingers ominously. He had won the right to slap the inside of your wrist with his fingers, and licking them allegedly intensified the pain. There was great danger, but there were, to my recollection, no fights.

There were no fights, but there was war.

There was a playing field behind the school where every winter the city dumped all the snow they scraped from the streets. By January the field rolled like the Plains of Abraham. The grade fours would occupy one of the snow hills and foolishly challenge the grade fives to throw them off. The wars, as Dane Lanken recalls, couldn't have been more Canadian. They were fought with snow.

"I remember massive snowball fights where it seems all the boys in the school would go and divide into two sides and throw snowballs at each other. And there would be waves of assaults across the fields and taking of prisoners and making little kids make snowballs for the big kids. It was real war. It was tremendously exciting. High adventure. And one winter I remember they announced that snowball fighting was no longer allowed in the school yard of Elizabeth Ballantyne School, and that seemed to be a great tragedy to everybody. It was the end of a friendly warfare that had probably gone on for many, many years. It also seems to me that this was the same time that TV came in, and hockey moved into arenas with helmets on, stuff like that, a general softening of boyhood. Removing adventure and danger from it. For better maybe, but maybe for worse."

I was the first person in the school yard that morning in my neighbourhood, and as it filled up with boys and balls, everything was hauntingly similar. The mood of anticipation, of shared secrets, was just the way I remembered. But many of the activities were strange to me. Organized. Slicker, somehow. I felt like a stranger, an interloper. And, though I had my tape recorder with me, I just stood in my corner and watched. I was the first there and the last to leave. I left without talking to anyone.

As I walked past the Korean grocery store on my way home, a boy with a knapsack slung sloppily over one shoulder galloped up the street towards me. The school yard had long ago emptied. Everyone had gone inside. I smiled and nodded as the boy stumbled by, but he was in too much of a hurry to notice me. One of his shoes had come undone and the lace was slapping the sidewalk as he ran. Grade four, I thought to myself. Late again.

THE ADVENTUROUS LIFE OF JOHN GODDARD

When John Goddard was fifteen years old, he sat down one night with a red pencil, a blue pen and a yellow legal pad and made a list of things he wanted to do before he died.

His list began just the way you might expect:

- Become an Eagle Scout.
- Broad jump fifteen feet.
- Make a parachute jump.
- Dive in a submarine.
- Learn ju-jitsu.

The more the boy wrote, the more his imagination took hold. The list soon left the realm of idle daydreams and entered the world of serious adolescent fantasy:

- Milk a poisonous snake.
- Light a match with a 22.
- Watch a fire-walking ceremony in Surinam.
- Watch a cremation ceremony in Bali.

And it didn't stop there. As young Goddard continued his list, his vision expanded and showed signs of the grand adventurer he was going to grow up to be:

- Explore the Amazon.
- Swim in Lake Tanganyika.
- Climb the Matterhorn.
- Retrace the travels of Marco Polo and Alexander the Great.
- Visit every country in the world.

The ideas poured onto the page and at some point took a sharp turn in tone. As Goddard added to his list, he displayed an academic sophistication well beyond his fifteen years:

- Read the works of Shakespeare, Plato, Aristotle, Dickens, Thoreau, Rousseau, Hemingway, Twain, Burroughs, Talmage, Tolstoy, Longfellow, Keats, Poe, Bacon, Whittier and Emerson.
- Become familiar with the compositions of Bach, Beethoven, Debussy, Ibert, Mendelssohn, Lalo, Milhaud, Ravel, Rimsky-Korsakov, Respighi, Rachmaninoff, Paganini, Stravinsky, Toch, Tchaikovsky, Verdi.
- Read the Bible from cover to cover.
- Play the flute and the violin.

When he put his pens down, there were 127 items on Goddard's list.

Well. Yes.

We have all taken a stab at this sort of thing at one time or another. The extraordinary difference between John Goddard and the rest of us, however, is the unsettling fact that Goddard didn't throw his list out. Nor did he chuck it into the bottom of a drawer. He kept his list in plain sight and set out to complete every item line by line. Today

Goddard has check marks beside 108 of his original 127 goals. And that includes all of the items mentioned above.

Well, that's not exactly true. There are still thirty odd countries that he hasn't visited. But he is working on that.

I first read about John Goddard in *Life* magazine when I was a teenager. It was in one of those articles at the back of the magazine in a section called the "Parting Shots". The article stuck in my mind (How could I forget it?) and I always hoped I would get a chance to talk to him. Fifteen years later I sat down with his phone number in front of me and called him at his home in La Cañada, California. I wanted to talk to him, I explained, about the list I had seen so long ago in *Life*. I wanted to know if he was still working on it. Yes, he was. Did he remember what had inspired him to write it? John Goddard chuckled.

"I think what motivated me to write the list was listening to some family friends who were visiting with my parents. They had been over for dinner and were helping to clear the dishes. I was doing my homework in a little alcove, a sort of breakfast nook. The man of the family, a Dr Keller, looked at me and said to my parents, 'I'd give anything to be John's age again. I really would do things differently. I would set out and accomplish more of the dreams of my youth.' That was the gist of his conversation – if only he could start over – and I thought, here's a man only forty-two years old, and he is feeling life has passed him by, and I thought, if I start planning now, and really work on my goals, I won't end up that way."

Almost fifty years have passed since John Goddard wrote out his life goals. He is now in his mid-sixties. But the day we spoke, he was busy preparing for a trip to the North Pole – one half of goal number 54, which is to visit both the North and the South poles. Another check mark. I spoke to John Goddard for almost two hours, and we talked about many things. I asked him if he remembered the day he wrote the list.

"I remember it vividly because it was such a rite of passage for me. It was a rainy Sunday afternoon in 1941. Until that time I really hadn't crystallized all my ambitions and hopes and dreams. Writing them down was the first act in achieving them. You know, when you write something down with the sincere intent of doing it, it's a commitment. A lot of us fail to do that. We don't set deadlines and say, for example, by June of 1990 I'm going to have checked out in scuba, taken a rock climbing course and learned how to play the piano. The moment of writing it down is vivid in my mind because that was my formal commitment to that life list. And I felt I would give myself a lifetime to fulfil everything on it."

One of Goddard's early challenges was an expedition by kayak down the longest river on earth – the 4,000-mile Nile. He was the first person in the world to travel the length of the river from the headwaters to the Mediterranean. He took a bank loan to finance the trip and then paid off the loan by writing a book about his adventures. He sold the book on the lecture circuit. And that's the way he has made his living ever since. Goddard supports himself through his lectures, his books, and the sale of his films and tapes. He is not a wealthy man.

I asked him if he had ever been in any physical danger. He told me of the time he was lost in a sand storm in the Sudan, and couldn't put up a tent because the wind was blowing so hard. But he couldn't sit still because if he had stopped moving, he would have been buried alive. He told me about the time he had been shot at by river pirates in Egypt. Later I read that he had also been bitten by a rattlesnake, charged by an elephant, trapped in quicksand, been in more than one plane crash and caught in more than one earthquake.

Sometimes I go on and on about a hazardous drive my family and I had one winter between Montreal and Toronto. It was snowing more than usual, the driving was tough, and there were a lot of cars off the road. There was also a service centre every fifty-odd miles, lots of snow-ploughs and plenty of people to help out if I had got in trouble. Nevertheless, when I tell the story of the drive I can make it sound pretty dramatic.

Imagine being able to start a story with "Exploring the Congo was difficult . . ."

"Exploring the Congo was difficult. It took me six months and resulted in the loss of life of my partner, Jack Yowell from Kenya. Four hundred miles down-stream we had a disaster when we both capsized on a raging stretch of rapids. It was the 125th set of rapids, and we were paddling fragile 60-pound, 16-foot kayaks. He got swept to the left and flipped over, and racing over to help him I got flipped over, too, and nearly drowned myself. I tried to fight to the surface and banged into the river bottom. The river was so turbulent I couldn't really tell which way the surface was, and I was drowning because I was under the water an interminable time. I think the thing that saved me was the fact that I could hold my breath for three minutes in an emergency. I was finally washed to calm water and ran along the banks desperately trying to find Jack. I couldn't see him anywhere. Then suddenly a box of matches came floating by, then his pipe, overturned kayak and aluminium paddle, but no Jack. It was very difficult to go on and travel the remaining 2,300 miles to the Atlantic. But we had promised one another if one of us did die on the upper river that the survivor would continue and finish the expedition for both of us. So I fulfilled that promise."

John Goddard still has a lot of things left on his list, but at age sixty-four he is in good shape and determined to keep at it. He does one hundred sit-ups every morning, works out on cables and weights and rides a stationary bike at least six miles a day.

Wanting a better measure of the man, I asked him what he has learned from all his travels.

Without missing a beat, Goddard began to talk about the destruction of the Brazilian rain forest. It was, he said, the most devastating ecological event on the globe. Then he interrupted himself.

"I think the most appalling thing I see is the chronic indifference of the world leaders to our critical problems of overpopulation and pollution. I'm not thinking of any individual leader, because they're all guilty of concentrating on profit and economic development. They seem to forget that just to exist is nothing. If you're surrounded by ugliness and pollution and you're not healthy and don't have a proper diet, what value is life? And you know our world is overpopulating at the rate of more than 85 million a year, and yet world leaders still don't seem to recognize the monumental threat imposed by human fertility. They still drag their feet and place one barrier after another in the way of meaningful population control. And as I travel around the world, just this summer, for example, I see Kenya so overpopulated that everyone's standard of living is brought down, and yet the approach to it is simplistic and bureaucratic. The future looks rather grim. Egypt is bursting at the seams with 52 million, and yet there is no serious effort to curb that population. Where are you going to put the people when the population starts doubling every twenty-five to thirty years. Mexico is in dire trouble right now, yet what little family planning they have is mere tokenism."

As we talked, I wondered whether Goddard thought he was going to be able to put a check mark beside all his goals. Would he get to the moon? Probably not. He should, I thought. Here he is, sixty-four years old and still learning. He recently checked off number 108 on his list by learning to play polo. How many years, I asked, did he think he had left?

"Oh, I'm still young. I'll make ninety. I'm in superb shape. In fact, my flight surgeon said my physiological profile fits right in with the pilots who are in their mid-thirties."

I asked him what he wanted on his tombstone, and he said he wanted them to write that he had been "Ruled by Love". Then I asked him how he thought he would die.

"Oh, probably in an attempt to go to Mars. I've always wanted to explore the river valleys of Mars and see if there are any fossils embedded in the sides of the canyons. Wouldn't you like to do that?"

Some weeks after we spoke on the telephone, I received a package in the mail from John Goddard. It was a motivational tape he sells and a brochure he sends around to people who want to book him for speaking engagements.

His picture was on the back of the brochure. He looked just the way you would want him to look. The way Indiana Jones should look. Like Errol Flynn or Ronald Coleman. He has dark hair and a black moustache and he doesn't look a day over forty. And I bet he can still hold his breath for three minutes under water. And if I was a smoker, and asked him for a light, and if he smiled and pulled out a 22, I wouldn't bat an eye.

THE NIGHT DENNIS LEE
ATE ALLIGATOR PIE

The words, written in chalk on the restaurant blackboard, were not ambiguous, but I looked a second time to make sure I had got it right. "Alligator Stew", it read. I signalled our waiter. I suspected this was just a cute *nom de guerre* someone had dreamed up for a vegetarian dish sculpted with cucumber and avocado. But there was always, God help me, the chance it was the real thing.

It was the real thing.

Honest-to-God alligator stew made with honest-to-God alligator meat.

I eat just about everything that is put in front of me, except, that is, for major league organs. I am not really sure what a sweetbread is, except I know it comes from either the top or bottom of the animal, and that, if you don't mind, is all I want to know about sweetbreads. I'm also not crazy about food with lumps, like Jell-O seasoned with pieces of fruit, or rice pudding, but I'll eat just about anything else. I have lost the instinctive aversion I had as a child to new and unfamiliar food.

Suddenly, sitting in the restaurant, I became a kid again.

"What's for dinner, Mom?"
"Alligator stew."
"I don't like alligator stew!"
"How do you know you don't like it? You've never tried it!"

My mother's voice rang in my ears as I placed my order.

I ordered the pasta.

How come I can eat cow but not horse? Pig but not dog? Lobster but not . . . alligator? As a kid I was comfortable with such inconsistencies. As an adult I wanted to know more.

I began my exploration of alligator stew the next morning. I returned to the kitchen of the restaurant where everything had begun and soon found out I wasn't the only person who had felt uncomfortable with the alligator stew. Paul Rooney, the sous chef at The Other Cafe, told me that while I had been wrestling with the concept out front, he had been having his own problems in the kitchen.

"I guess I was a touch nervous, because I've made stews before, but never an alligator stew. I tasted it, and it tasted all right to me, but I wasn't sure how the customers were going to respond. When the first order came in, Mike yelled, 'We've got an alligator stew order,' and I ran up to the front and made sure it was put on the plate and garnished properly and so on. We had a last look at it and it was sent out and then we had some very apprehensive moments. I was trying to imagine what this fellow looked like who was eating it, and wondering if he was an exotic-food connoisseur or something. Several hundred questions kept going through my head. When the comment came back to the kitchen that the stew was good, everyone went 'Thank God', you know."

The mood in the kitchen had, apparently, lightened up considerably after that first order. Paul told me that the kitchen staff spent the rest of the night joking about alligators, and that told me they were still feeling slightly uneasy about the whole thing.

My next stop was not far from the restaurant. I went to see the man who had imported the alligator meat to Toronto. His name is Michael Vaughan. He runs a fish business known as Michael's Mussels and was anxious to convince me that not only was alligator meat delicious, it was good for me to boot.

"It has a mild taste because it is low in fat. It is less than $1^1/2$ percent fat, and it's very high in protein and very low in calories. An average dinner portion would have about 230 calories, so that's a pretty nutritious item."

There is, he told me, currently about 150,000 pounds of alligator meat being "harvested" every year in Louisiana. On an annual basis that works out to one hundredth of an ounce of meat for every person living in the United States. You don't have to be a statistician to figure out that if the stuff ever catches on, there is a serious supply problem brewing, which is why I decided my next stop had to be Louisiana.

It wasn't so long ago that spotting an alligator in Louisiana was something to talk about. Alligators were nearly extinct, and actually on the state endangered list, until they rebounded recently and the wildlife authorities introduced a hunt. September is alligator season in the bayous. During September each licensed hunter is given a controlled number of 'gator tags. They can bag one alligator per tag. Ellis Benckenstein hunts 'gators for money; this year he was allotted fifty-one tags. Working alone, Ellis "tagged out" in eight days, which is a lot more 'gators than I'd bring back in a week if you threw me in a boat the size of a dining-room table and sent me out in a Louisiana swamp by myself.

When I spoke to Ellis, I wanted to know just how he caught 'gators. Basically, he fishes for them.

"The best bait we've found is chicken. We either use a drumstick or a thigh or a piece of breast meat. The line is set up so the bait is ten inches out of the water. We hang it out of the water so the crabs and turtles won't take it. You set your lines one day and go back the next morning and check your lines and when you catch one, well, hell, it'll be at the end of the line and you've got to wrassle with him to get him up where you can shoot him. It's like having a Brahma bull on the end of a rope, or a cow. And until they play out you can't get them up or get them close to you. We try to shoot them right behind the head where there's a bulge in the vertebrae system."

The bayous have always had their share of freelance operators like Ellis, who hunt 'gators the way their pappies taught them. With the reintroduction of the hunt, however, the freelancers have witnessed a whole alligator industry pop up around the state. We are talking alligator infrastructure complete with alligator farms and alligator processing plants. I talked to Keith Myers, who butchers 'gators in a place called Palmetto, Louisiana.

"Our plant is a building forty feet by sixty feet, full of big aluminum tables. We put a whole 'gator on each table to be deboned. We have a crew of ladies who work on the tail section, and we have some that work on the rest of the body. It's a very tedious job to take the meat off an alligator because there are pockets of fat that have to be removed if you want to have a good-quality product. The meat is separated into different grades. We have one that is strictly a tail filet, and it's used mainly for frying or sautéing. And then we have mixed filet which is from the rest of the body, which you use in soups and stews and sausage."

According to both Keith and Ellis, people in their neighbourhood eat 'gator as often as I eat chicken. They fry it, poach it, and even grind it up and make patties out of it. Ellis says 'gator meat is a regular part of his diet.

Which left me feeling a touch foolish.

Time, I thought, to return to The Other Cafe and take my inhibitions, once again, to the cutting edge of journalism. All food writers take a companion with them when they write about restaurants, and I didn't see why I should be any different. I knew there was only one person in Canada who'd fit the bill – Canada's reptilian rhymer, the man who doomed himself to joining me by penning the immortal lines:

Alligator pie, alligator pie,
If I don't get some I think I'm gonna die.
Give away the green grass, give away the sky,
But don't give away my alligator pie.

I had already met Dennis Lee once or twice before I phoned to extend my invitation. We live in the same neighbourhood and have mutual friends. I introduced myself briefly and said I had reservations for the two of us to go out and eat . . . alligator.

There was a pause.
Dennis hesitated.
Then he said, "What time do I have to be there?"
I thought I spotted a hint of enthusiasm in his voice.

When we met at the restaurant the next evening, Dennis seemed quite excited. I told him that in honour of his appearance the chef had taken the remainder of the alligator stew and baked it in a pie crust. We were actually about to eat an Alligator Pie.

We were sitting at a small table near a window waiting for the pie to arrive when Dennis suddenly leaned forward and quietly confided that he had written a new poem to mark the moment. He looked around the restaurant and then reached into his pocket and pulled out a crumpled piece of paper. This is what he read to me.

Alligator pie, alligator pie,
I sidled down to Bloor Street and thought
  I'd have a try.
I'd put it in a verse, but I ate it with a sigh:
"What the heck am I doing trying to make myself gobble
  up a real live Alligator Pie?"

Our soups came first. I had the zucchini vegetable, Dennis had the lentil.
And then they brought IT out.
I looked down at my plate and then slowly over at Dennis. He was poking at his plate with a fork the way you might poke at a dead squirrel.
I looked back at my plate.
It looked just like quiche.
It came with cauliflower and baby boiled potatoes.
Dennis was wolfing down his cauliflower. He stopped and grinned sheepishly. His fork hovered over his plate

like the sword of death. Then he shrugged and took a
piece of pie and put it carefully into his mouth so that
none of it touched his lips. He looked at me accusingly. I
did the same.

It tasted just like the chicken pot pie they used to serve
in my school cafeteria.

Chicken pot pie!

Later I asked Dennis what he had been thinking during
those moments when the pie was sitting in front of him.

"To tell you the truth I felt spooked, I really did. I
guess a lot of it has to do with eating an unfamiliar
animal. I'm not sensitive on the subject of eating
animal meat, but any time I feel that I've eaten the
meat of a new animal, there's a sense of infringing on
new territory, and some sense of a mild taboo being
broken. It's the same feeling that most North Americans have, for example, if they find out that they've
eaten horse meat. Most of us will recoil, even though
in some parts of the world it is as common as eating
the meat of a cow is for us. There is a sense of
tiptoeing across a taboo. But I lived to tell the tale, or
regurgitate the tale, and . . . it's not bad. There was
nothing disagreeable about the flavour whatsoever.
All the images you might have of scales and jaws have
nothing to do with what you taste. It was very
palatable. It was much more delicate than you would
expect when you think about the appearance of an
alligator. As alligators go I found it – how can I put
this – I'd say it had a cheeky little bouquet. There was
a bit of nose to it, I thought, but probably more of a
tail. But on balance I would speak strongly for it."

At this point the evening took on a certain festive twist.
Michael from Michael's Mussels arrived and announced

he was going to start selling alligator meat in his store down on Harbord Street. He asked Dennis to come down and do a book signing to inaugurate the occasion. Jeff, the chef at The Other Cafe, joined our table in his white uniform and said he would serve alligator stew every Thursday night for a while. Some friends joined us, and we drank too much wine and carried on until late at night.

I haven't been back since. Nor have I opened the container of frozen alligator meat Michael gave me. It's still downstairs in the freezer. I am not sure I'll ever cook it now. But I can't bring myself to throw it out. There is something about having an alligator in my freezer that adds a certain charm to the search for the leg of lamb.

IN PRAISE OF THE POPSICLE

The Popsicle, it turns out, was invented quite accidentally, by an eleven-year-old boy. Frank Epperson had his collision with fate in northern California around the turn of the century. The fateful moment (for Frank, and for mankind, as it turned out), was largely due to a fluke in the weather. Fluke or not, today, executives of Popsicle Industries at Popsicle corporate headquarters in Englewood, New Jersey, make no bones about saluting Frank Epperson as the father of the Popsicle. I know this because I heard it from Popsicle executive Alan von Kreuter.

"It was 1905 and Epperson had mixed some then-popular soda water powder and left it outside overnight with a stirring stick in it. The temperature dropped to a record low that night and the next morning when he came out he had a-frozen-product-on-a-stick. It took about fifteen years for Frank to recognize the commercial value of his invention, but when he did, he got a patent for it, and once he had the patent, he started selling it at carnivals on the west coast – but he wasn't doing a grand job of it."

Frank didn't call his invention the Popsicle, of course. He called it, understandably enough, the Epsicle. He made a modest living selling hotdogs, popcorn and his Epsicle out of the back of a trailer that he lugged around the west coast carnival circuit. He continued like that until 1925 when a baker from New York City, Joe Lowe, walked into his life and history.

Before I get too far along here, perhaps I should declare my position. I hold that among the millions of manufactured items available in the world today, the Popsicle shines out as a beacon of perfection.

I don't believe the Popsicle could be improved upon. You couldn't dip a Popsicle in chocolate or roll it in nuts. This wouldn't make it more exotic. It would make it silly. You couldn't change its shape. The shape – part art deco, part space age – is, well, perfect. Nor would you want to change the wooden stick. Popsicle Industries made the mistake of trying that a few years ago and, to their chagrin, learned the hard way that plastic sticks are too smooth for their product. A Popsicle mounted on a plastic stick tends to slip off the stick. Even the packaging is perfect. The red, white and blue colours? Perfect. The cycle ball? Perfect. Everything, right down to the feel of the paper is perfect. The Popsicle is a perfect product in an imperfect age. A touchstone to the past.

Popsicles are even consumed in perfection. Kids use the Popsicle the way an Inuit hunter uses a seal. Nothing is wasted. They eat the frozen part, build with the sticks and trade the packaging to amass material goods.

A Popsicle is unpretentious. The Popsicle was perfected in the 1920s and no one has felt compelled to renovate, redesign or retrofit it for over fifty years, and that is something to take note of. Your friends may have deserted you, your spouse who promised to stick around till death did you part has probably shipped off, the neighbourhood is no longer the same; but you can walk into any corner store in the country today and – OK, OK, it will be a little more expensive and a little smaller, but – you can buy a piece of the past.

Now, where was I? Oh, yes. Joe Lowe.

Joe owned a bakery in New York City.

Now, people don't buy a lot of baked goods in the summer time, so in 1925, Joe happened to be roaming around California looking for something he could add to his line that would do well in the hotter months. When he saw the . . . uh . . . Epsicle, he knew right away that he had found what he was looking for. Joe Lowe was about to become for the Epsicle what Ray Kroc would later be for the hamburger.

The first thing Joe did was buy the rights for the frozen confection from Frank Epperson, who exits from our narrative here. Joe then took the Epsicle to the national market, though not without modifications. First, the name "Epsicle" was retired and "Popsicle" ushered in. The new name was a neat combination of "pop" from "lollipop", and "icle" from "icicle". Joe also changed the shape of the Epsicle.

> "The original stick confections were made in a round, long sort of test-tube type shape. The twin Popsicle was born during the Depression. The problem then was that a lot of people didn't have adequate funds to give their children constant nickels for candy, particularly if they had a multiple child family. The concept was developed so the Popsicle could be split and shared between two children

for a nickel. That was the development of the twin
Popsicle."

The only thing that has changed since the Depression is
the Popsicle's size. It used to be 4 ounces. Somewhere
along the line it was reduced to 3 ounces. When metric
came in they sneaked it down to 2.6 ounces. Otherwise it
hasn't changed one iota. It is exactly the same product
that it was in 1930.

Although it has been a beacon of stability, I don't want
to give the impression that the development of the
Popsicle has been all smooth sailing. It is just that the
Popsicle people seem divinely guided. Just about everything they do works out – even their mistakes, like the
origin of the blue ones.

"We were trying to make raspberry and what happened was that somebody put the wrong colour in
the batch. It was just a question of colour. Everything else, like the flavour, was fine, it was raspberry.
But they forgot to put the red colour in. There was
supposed to be a *little* blue in there, and instead of
the red and blue combination they put all blue. We
sent it to the stores and it was called Sky Blue and it
was a phenomenon. We had tremendous success with
it. So we had to leave it that colour."

While I was talking to von Kreuter on the telephone, I was
suddenly seized by the urge to see how Popsicles are
made. So I arranged to visit a Popsicle plant and watched
in awe thousands of Popsicles marching down an assem-
bly line like little frozen soldiers.

They totter upside down along a conveyor belt and
through a freezer in aluminium moulds with their sticks
waggling gamely in the air until they freeze in place. At
Canadian corporate headquarters in Burlington, Ontario,

I marvelled at pallets of chocolate and jugs of flavour concentrate that reached to the sky. Dave Dotson, who works for Popsicle Canada, says that like everything else, Canadians have evolved regional differences in Popsicle taste.

"Take root beer. Root beer is a very unusual flavour. Historically it has sold like mad in the saltwater areas of the east and west coasts and hardly moved at all in central Canada. As a result it is probably the number three flavour in the Maritimes and in British Columbia. But is not even carried for the most part throughout the middle part of the country.

"Several years ago we realized that we had such a large Italian population in the city of Toronto that we thought it might be an idea to bring out a white lemon or an Italian ice type of Popsicle and give it a try here in the city, which we did. It rapidly became a very popular flavour in the Ontario market-place. Quebec has always been partial to strawberry Popsicles, and although it doesn't enjoy much popularity anywhere else in the country, it is a very strong flavour there."

As I was about to leave the Burlington headquarters, Mr. Dotson asked me if I would like to meet Popsicle Pete. I had never even thought to ask.

Her name is Jean Kerr.

Popsicle Pete is a girl.

Jean works alone in a room the size of a classroom. As I wandered through her little warehouse, I let my hand brush against boxes of premiums that felt and looked so familiar. There was the pile of Popsicle towels, the box of Frisbees and the shelves of T-shirts. When I came across the box of Popsicle suspenders in the far corner, however,

I stopped short. I had wanted a pair of Popsicle suspenders since I first saw them advertised on the back of a Popsicle wrapper. That was a lifetime ago, and I still wanted them.

"Go ahead," said Jean, watching me as I picked up a pair. "Don't be shy."

I couldn't quite believe what was happening to me. Premiums I had once dreamed of were stacked around me on shelves that almost reached the ceiling. I felt like an art lover let loose in the Louvre. And now Popsicle Pete herself had just told me to pocket a pair of suspenders.

Clutching the suspenders, I walked over to Jean, who was sorting the mail. I asked her if a lot of people wrote.

"We get bundles of mail every day. Maybe as many as two or three hundred letters. People write and want to know how old I am, and if I'm a boy or a girl. I sort of don't answer that one; I let that go by the board. And I've never had an answer back saying, you didn't tell me if you were a girl or a boy. There are people who write all the time. We have one chap in Winnipeg who writes almost twice a week, and we don't know whether he's a child or an adult. In fact, we got two letters from him today. I can tell they're from him as soon as I see the envelope. We don't have too many city people writing in. It's mostly rural folks, mainly, I think, because they don't have a Collegiate Sport or a Woolco or whatever, and they don't mind writing in for things and waiting three weeks to get them. But city kids, they seem to have to go to the store right now and get it today sort of thing. The guy from Winnipeg usually wants crazy straws or pens. We just don't know what on earth he does with all the pens he gets from us. But he just keeps writing for pens and crazy straws. He maybe gets a hundred pens a year. I don't know, maybe he gives them away. He's been writing for maybe four years, maybe longer."

One summer I saved Popsicle wrappers in a cardboard box under my bed. I was saving for the suspenders. You could send three wrappers plus $3.35, and Popsicle Pete would send you the suspenders. But for one thousand wrappers you got the suspenders for free. The challenge appealed to me, and I asked all my friends to bring me their wrappers which I flattened out and stored in a box under by bed. I nearly got enough. But something happened and I never sent away. One thousand wrappers is a mighty big pile of wrappers, and I remember wondering how I would ever get them in a mailbox. There were easily more wrappers under my bed than you could fit in a couple of large shopping bags.

I asked Jean if people ever did send in wrappers for the free prizes, or whether they just sent the money.

"Most of them send the money," she said.

"When they send the wrappers," I asked, "do you count them?"

"Of course I do," she said, laughing.

"Of course," I said.

THE SHOCKING TRUTH ABOUT HOUSEHOLD DUST

S o. From time to time I joke about being out on the cutting edge of journalism. If pressed, however, I would be the first to admit that the majority of what I seem to end up writing about lies well off the beaten track. I try hard to follow world events. I do. But it is a struggle. I am easily distracted by those bits in my newspaper about the parrot who has been taught to whistle a Chopin sonata by the out-of-work conductor. And once I have read something like that, I just can't help myself.

This can be a problem for somebody like me who counts among his friends a number of this country's distinguished journalists. We go out for lunch together, my friends and I, and they will argue for hours about the implications of their upcoming interview with the minister of finance, while I push at my salad and silently ponder my profile of the Popsicle, or the history of the Yo-Yo. I leave these lunches determined to do something journalistically credible before I see anyone again.

Such was my mood on an otherwise pleasant Tuesday

afternoon several years ago. I would, I seethed, storming through the Yonge Street lunch crowd with my elbows just a little too far from my sides, uncover a real story. In this frame of investigative frenzy I returned to my desk and, unfortunately, fell into a telephone conversation with my friend Robert Krulwich of CBS about ... dust. Common household dust. As usual, Krulwich had some questions that neither of us could answer. Dust questions.

Like how come the dust on the top of your refrigerator lies there like a layer of velvet, while the stuff under your bed rolls around like tumbleweeds in the interior of British Columbia? And the little specks in the sunbeam, are they floating or falling? And where does dust come from, anyway? How come you can vacuum your heart out one day and the next morning there'll be a dust bunny in the cupboard?

As the afternoon wore on, my need to know the answer to these and other puzzles overtook whatever it was I was supposed to be doing. I should have known better, but I shrugged and reached for the phone. What follows is the weird and shocking truth I discovered that day about household dust. Like all good stories it begins at the beginning.

Ever wonder where dust comes from? How about outer space? There is extraterrestrial dust in your living-room. Probably not a lot of it, but it is there, and I offer that up at the beginning as a kind of warning, because this is going to get a lot weirder before we are finished. Space dust comes from meteorites. When meteorites strike the earth's atmosphere they disintegrate and turn to, you guessed it, dust, increasing the bulk of our planet, incidentally, by 10,000 tons a year. I am told by eminent scientists who study dust that if you were to run your finger along a window ledge somewhere, anywhere, you are almost certain to pick up some dust from outer space.

I learned about space dust from a Dr John Ferguson, who is a dust scientist for Bristol-Myers. They are the folks who produce, among other things, Endust, so he should know. He did assure me that meteorites are not the major cause of the dust in my house.

"We create an awful lot of dust by our daily living inside the house, the most common thing being, of course, through our cooking and our grooming habits, or the clothes that we wear. Also, there's the normal wearing away of the interior of the house – paint chipping off, bits of paper coming from wallpaper, things like that."

In fact, the majority of the dust in your house comes from the house itself and everything in it, wearing away. The same thing happens outdoors. There is a lot of concrete dust floating around, for example. Every time someone drives down the road, tiny bits of road are knocked off, and these microscopic bits float away and become specks of dust on someone's basement window. There is also rubber dust that comes from the tires that are busy wearing away the street, and chances are they will end up on the same basement window.

To these normal, everyday happenings you have to add something called "dust events" – things like volcanic eruptions, forest fires and other natural phenomena that spew ash into the atmosphere.

But that's not all – a significant amount of the dust in your home is, in fact, made up of little bits and pieces of you. In this way, you are no different from the wallpaper in your bathroom. The outermost layer of your skin is known as the stratum corneum. You shed your stratum corneum every three days, just like a snake. That's about fifty thousand skin cells. Or so says Dr Charles McLeod, a pathologist from Washington, D.C., who recently studied dust for *Discover* magazine.

> "If you brush through your hair in the right light, you can see small flecks of dander or dandruff that flake off your scalp, and this process is continuous on all the skin surfaces of your body. People are constantly shedding little flakes of dead skin. It is a normal process."

Now we come to the good part. Having established where dust comes from, it is time to take a closer look at dust itself. This is the part that upsets people. If you are squeamish about these sorts of things you might consider putting this book away now. There are only a few pages left anyway and you might be better off, happier, more relaxed just not knowing abut this next bit.

Don't say I didn't warn you. There are, uh, animals that live in the dust in your house. Millions and millions of animals. They are called dust mites. And they may be tiny, but they are the most horrible little creatures you can imagine. They feed on floating bits of skin. They suck in air through their toes. And they look like monsters from outer space. Don't take my word for it. Dr McLeod has actually looked at dust mites, face to face, through a microscope.

> "They have these very large mouth parts that allow them to chew their food. And depending on the stage at which you look at them, they may have up to eight legs. Have you ever seen a lobster? Have you ever seen a cockroach? Well, imagine breeding those two and looking at their offspring, and you have a good idea of what dust mites look like. They're not insects,

now, they're mites. Insects only have six legs. Nobody has ever counted, but you could estimate that there are millions of mites per square yard of space. They don't take up a whole lot of room. They don't make any noise, so you'd never know they're there. If you accumulated enough of them and you bunched them together, you could see them with the naked eye. I'd say it would take a couple of dozen to cover the head of a pin, though."

Dust mites can walk on their hideous eight legs, but for a mite to travel, say, across the room, would be roughly the equivalent of you setting off from Moose Jaw to walk to Come-by-Chance to pick up the morning paper. So you can understand why mites don't do a lot of walking. What they like to do is ride air currents. Every time you take a deep breath and blow it out, you're helping a bunch of mites get around.

The good news about these little beasts is that they won't touch you, and they won't eat you. Dr Edward Baker is an acarologist in Alabama (which means that he studies mites, Alabaman or otherwise). He once took a garbage pail full of mites and taped them, under capsules, to various parts of his arm. He was prepared to let them nosh away to their hearts' delight on his stratum cor-neum, but when he took off the tape, they were all dead. Apparently, dust mites only go after the bits and pieces that slough off. That's the good news.

The bad news about dust mites is that they have normal bodily functions. Twenty times a day each mite produces a mite pellet. When people say they are allergic to dust, they really mean they are allergic to things in the dust. It might be pollen – there is a lot of pollen in dust – but it could be that they are allergic to mite poop.

There is no getting around dust mites. As long as you keep sloughing off, as long as there is dust, there are going to be mites. If you have a vacuum cleaner in your closet, there are, right now, in the bag with the dust, millions of mites, grazing happily. Turn on the vacuum and the mites go turtle. They pull their hideous lobster legs into their hideous bodies and wait until you have finished. Then they come out again and graze. Tonight when you climb into bed, you will be sharing it with about two million dust mites. So you might as well start thinking about them as your friends, because there is nothing else you can do about them.

Another thing you can do nothing about is the dust that floats in the sunbeam. I used to wonder if I left the house quietly and let the air get real still, whether all that dust would settle, and I could sneak back in and vacuum it up before it started floating again. Dr Ferguson set me straight.

"The larger particles are actually falling. But if the particles are small enough, the movement of the air is sufficient to keep them suspended. A layman's way of looking at that is if you toss a tin can into the air and you shoot at it with a bullet, you can keep that can suspended indefinitely so long as you can keep hitting it with a bullet. Essentially, if you have a particle of dust that is light enough, the movement of the air molecules behave just like the bullets from that gun. They will keep bouncing into the dust particle and keep it suspended."

Some dust particles are so light that a simple wave of your hand or even the cat walking across the kitchen will send them swirling up. And there it stays, unless, of course, the dust was to meet its mortal enemy – rain. Dust hates rain. It loves safe places where, through friction or electro-static energy or, best of all, grease, it can cling to other bits of dust and fulfil its *raison d'être* – become a dust ball. Since grease is dust's best friend, dust's favourite place is, of course, the kitchen. And in the kitchen, says Dr Ferguson, the place where dust reigns supreme is . . .

" . . . usually behind your refrigerator, or in the circulating fan above your stove or range. It accumulates on the fan because it is so close to the stove where the cooking fats and oils are volatilized. The grease sticks to the blades of the fan and the dust sticks to the grease. Your refrigerator works the same way because it's constantly recirculating the air in back of the coils for cooling. That will collect the fats and the oils and serve as a good sticking place for the dust as well."

And that, more or less, is the story of dust. Some of it might have upset you, but there's not much you can do about it. You could dust more, I guess, or dust better, but it won't do much good. Better just to accept it. Come to terms with the dust in your life. Remember that it is someone's home (ugly they may be, malevolent they are not). It contains matter from outer space. And, after all, you put a lot of yourself into making it.

ACKNOWLEDGEMENTS

Gloria Bishop was the executive producer of "Morningside" in 1984, and it was her idea that I start writing weekly essays for the show. This book would never have happened if Gloria hadn't called.

I have had a number of producers at "Morningside" over the years. Susan Perly, Tom MacDonnell and Nancy Watson helped me with the pieces in this book. They were always patient and full of good advice. They always made my work better. Catherine Yolles was responsible for getting me to Penguin. My editor Iris Skeoch held my hand once I got there, and Shelley Tanaka made sure I got more than the commas in the right places. Iris and Shelley deserve a big thanks.

Pete and Maggie Groves gave me their kitchen table to work on when I needed it, as did my friends Kris and Danny Finkleman. Two students at Ryerson, Jamie Robertson and Joe Ruttle, helped transcribe tape clips. Gail Donald and Ken Puley at CBC Radio archives helped us find the clips so we could get to work. Thanks also to Christeen Chidley-Hill, Alice Hopton, David Johnston,

Peter Livingston, Paul McLaughlin, Don Obe, Larry Scanlon, Peter Sibbald-Brown, Ken Wolff, Hal Wake and Jean Wright, who all offered valuable advice at various times.

To whatever extent these essays worked on the radio, I know to a large extent that they worked because of Peter Gzowski. His curiosity and generosity have been the foundation of our Monday morning get-togethers. If it wasn't for the patience of my wife, Linda, and the support of my producers, I'd say I owed this to him. Peter wrote part of this book, and I am proud to work with him and on his show.

I'd like to thank Linda especially – for putting up with my anxieties when the stories weren't working and sharing the fun when they were. Whenever I was stuck on Sunday nights, Linda was always around with good ideas.

Finally, I have dedicated this book to my parents. I guess I am trying to say the same thing to them as I am to all the people I have already mentioned. Thanks for the help. If I never said it before, I appreciate it. I am grateful.